A GEEK IN KOREA

DISCOVERING ASIA'S NEW KINGDOM OF COOL

DANIEL TUDOR

TUTTLE Publishing
Tokyo | Rutland, Vermont | Singapore

Contents

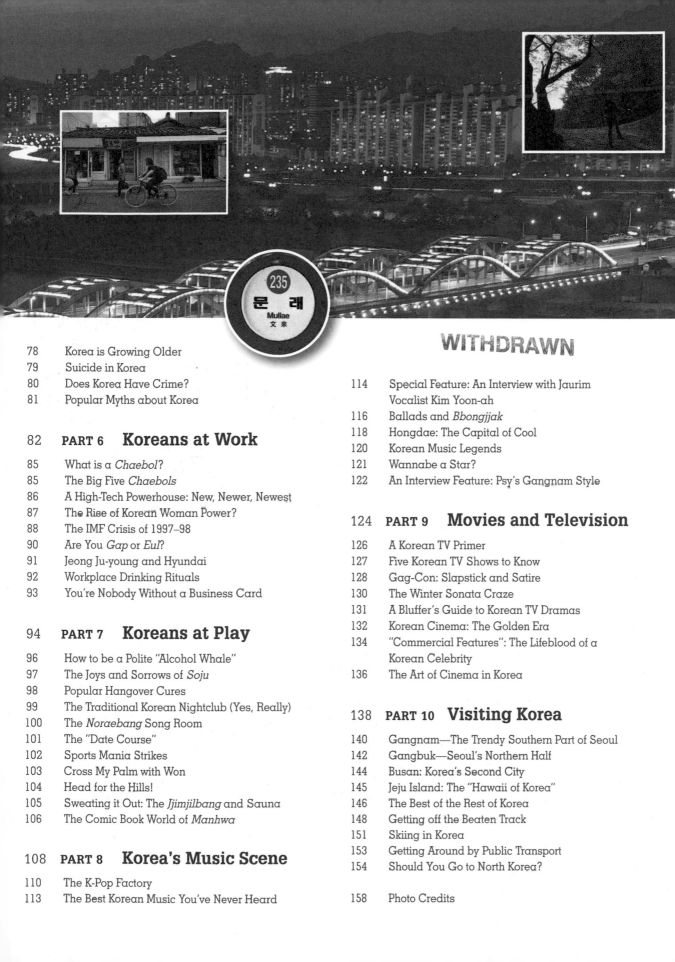

235
문 래
Mullae
文 来

WITHDRAWN

THE RISE OF COOL KOREA

"Korea? But there's a war going on there, isn't there?"
"Korea? Do you mean the North, or the South?"

These were the kind of reactions I got when I first told people I was going to live in Korea. They knew about the Korean War; they knew about the dictator in Pyongyang so memorably rendered in *Team America: World Police*; and, they also "knew" that dog-eating was a "common practice;" "Remember, Danny: a dog is for life, not just Christmas dinner," wrote one old friend in a card sent to me for the 2004 holiday season.

But something has changed. In the past decade or so, Korea—and by "Korea," I am referring to the South—has become cool. Though still off the radar for many Westerners, inbound tourist numbers have rocketed; creative exports like computer games, pop music, movies, and even the odd novel, have gained international attention in a way that no one here would have dared imagine at the turn of the millennium.

Around Asia, Korean "idol" stars are greeted with Beatlemania-style levels of hysteria. Actors like Bae Yong-joon are worshipped by legions of Japanese housewives.

The new face of Korea? There are few people in the world who don't recognize Psy, of "Gangnam Style" fame. His charmingly silly image has provided a great counterpoint to traditional conceptions of Korea, which center on the Korean War and industrial development.

And a critical blog post about a top Korean pop group's latest single will draw from overseas fans the kind of wrath that I would reserve for someone who had just gravely insulted my mother.

In the days of its rapid development, Korea inevitably had a rather gray, industrial image. Celebrities are now adding color, but this is only half the story. Today, a student toting a heavy bag full of textbooks might also have a guitar slung over his shoulder. Particularly around the Hongik University area of Seoul, there has been a flowering of "indie" culture. The bars and cafes there are full of people whose dreams are of rock n' roll, rather than of working for Samsung. They are driving "cool Korea" just as much as any actor with fancy hair.

But even if the Korean hipster isn't sure about becoming "Samsung Man," there's still a good chance Samsung will have made the phone in his pocket. Korean firms are now overtaking Japanese rivals and dominating markets worldwide in all types of funky gadgets. Hyundai cars used to be something of a joke in the US, but now they win awards. And in defiance of the risk aversion of their parents' generation, a new breed of high-tech start-up entrepreneur is emerging.

But why is all this happening? Is it just a matter of coincidence that Koreans suddenly seem to be making internationally successful music and movies, as well as the mp3 players and flat-screen TVs on which we appreciate them? Is it the result of a new focus on style and quality now the develop-at-all-costs philosophy of the past half century is finally subsiding? Is it the result of the political democratization of the past 25 years? Or is it, as cultural commentator and TV presenter Park Jung-sook says, simply Korea's turn to shine?

My cop-out answer is all of the above. But it is a pleasure to watch it all unfold, and a privilege to be able to write about it. I will consider this book a job well done if I can convince you to come here and see it all for yourself. So, I hope to see you in Seoul!

Falling in Love with a Country

There are many reasons why people come to this country. Some come for work, others come for marriage, and there are even those who are so obsessed with a particular Korean TV star or pop group that they pack up their things and move to Seoul. These days, there are also a few who have noticed "cool Korea" and want to get in on it. But for me, it all started with a sporting event.

I first set foot in Korea on the day the national football team played Italy in the 2002 World Cup. We'd been on the move for well over fifteen hours, in a journey that took in two plane rides and a bumpy trek in a car up the coast from Busan to the industrial city of Ulsan. Shattered, we stood at the check-in desk, waiting for service. The staff had no interest in helping us. They were watching TV: the match had gone to extra time, and it was made clear that everything had to wait until that deciding golden goal sailed beyond the outstretched hands of an agonized goalkeeper. When it did—courtesy of Korea's famed pretty-boy striker Ahn Jung-hwan—the joy that erupted was of the like of which I had never seen before. In the lobby of our five-star hotel, people dressed in red t-shirts, red bandanas, and with red face paint on, were bouncing in every direction. (continued on next page)

They crashed into each other, into us, and into pillars. They scattered chairs, and whatever hotel furniture dared stand in their way. They screamed and hugged with abandon. Despite being tired (and British), we became swept up in the tide of emotion. So we drank, danced, and yelled along with these overjoyed Korean fans for the rest of the day. We'd never seen them before, and would never see them again. The language barrier meant we couldn't even communicate properly. But for that one day, it felt like we'd known them all our lives.

It was like that for the rest of the tournament. We'd wander around Seoul carrying a ball, and strangers would challenge us to a game in the street. We'd then proceed to get drunk on *soju* (an alcoholic spirit) with them afterwards. It was a time of overwhelming humanity: everyone was your friend, and there were no barriers between people. Entire offices packed

up and went out into the streets. Bar owners would say, "here, have some more drinks on the house!" Normal rules were completely suspended, but nobody did you any harm.

I knew that the "World Cup spirit" couldn't last forever. But I also knew that there must have been something special about a country that could produce such an atmosphere. So I made up my mind to return. Now I work here, Korea has become "normal" to me—but the occasional burst of dynamic devil-may-care fun or act of great kindness from a stranger reminds me of why I first came to like this place so much.

I am also lucky to have built some extraordinary friendships here. Korea is certainly not a country without problems—many of which are covered in this book—but at the heart of its culture lies a redeeming warmth and humanity that is hard to find anywhere else.

KOREA: IT'S DIFFERENT

Every time I walk past a street vendor selling silkworm larvae as a snack, I'm reminded that "Korea is different." But it isn't just different in that "exotic" or "eastern" kind of way. Certainly, Korea has plenty in common with its neighbors, as can be expected; but those who think Korea is "just like China" or "just like Japan" are badly mistaken.

The main reason why Korean TV drama series are popular around Asia is that they are full of raw emotion. Unlike in Japan, where self-control is a social necessity, Koreans can be refreshingly direct with how they feel towards you. Whether those feelings are of love, anger, or indifference, you won't need to scratch your head wondering which. Due to a tendency for passionate and expressive behavior, Koreans are sometimes compared (and sometimes compare themselves) to the Italians.

Another stereotype with some degree of truth is that of Koreans as "the Irish of the East." This is not just due to the statistical fact that Koreans are by far the biggest drinkers in East Asia. For centuries, Koreans have been known as lovers of

My Life in Korea
When I first moved to Seoul, I taught English. Since then, I've been an investment manager, and a journalist at *The Economist*. These days, I'm an independent writer, and co-owner of The Booth, a craft beer business. The gentleman with me in the picture above is Kim Chang-wan, leader of Sanullim, one of Korea's best-loved rock bands. One of the best aspects of being a bar-owner is the ability to meet interesting people from all walks of life!

singing and dancing. Collectively, the Korean culture of drinking, singing, and dancing is known as *eumjugamu*. The word has negative connotations to some Koreans, but for me, it is one of the most attractive and defining aspects of Korean culture.

There also exists what I call a "natural socialism" in Korean culture. Even when individual portions are served in a restaurant, friends will move their plates into the center of the table, and share everything. "Every man for himself"—as found in today's China—is not a popular concept in Korea. Social inequality, though increasing, is considered a problem to be tackled rather than an inevitability to be accepted; even Korea's most conservative politicians feel compelled to confront this.

Korea is also a land of sad extremes. Proportionally, this country is world number one in terms of suicide, plastic surgery, and expenditure on "bling bling" luxury goods. It also

has probably the world's most stressed-out, over-burdened schoolchildren. All these are results of Korea's intense culture of competition, which makes it unacceptable to be merely good-looking, well-off, and well-educated. One must compete with others to be the best-looking, best-off, and best-educated.

It sounds like a total contradiction to say that Koreans are natural socialists who love drinking and partying, and yet are engaged in a vicious cycle of be-all-you-can-be competition against each other. But it isn't wrong. Korea is a complicated place of joy and tragedy, of fulfilment and frustration. You can at least be certain that it will never bore you.

Gwanghwamun The gate of Gwanghwamun in front of Gyeongbok Palace in Seoul is the focal point of the country. The nation's *gi* (energy) is said to flow through it.

PART 1 # KOREAN IDENTITY

Don't know your *jeong* from your *aegyo*?
Let's take a look at some of the most important
social traits and concepts that help make
modern Korea what it is today.

THE CONCEPTS OF *JEONG, HAN,* AND *HEUNG* UNIQUELY KOREAN CULTURAL CODES?

"My company runs on *jeong,*" says the chairman of one of Korea's ten largest conglomerates. A person considered to have a large capacity for *jeong* is probably well-liked. But according to a saying, *jeong* is also "the scariest thing." What on earth does this strange word mean, then?

I sometimes call *jeong* "the invisible hug." *Jeong* is a bond that exists between people, and gives them a sense of mutual destiny. If you share *jeong* with someone, then you ought to go the extra mile for them. You may even feel the need to bend or break society's rules to help that person.

Jeong isn't merely a matter of friendship. It can exist between members of large groups: Koreans are liable to helping graduates of the same school, university, hometown, or military unit as themselves, because of *jeong.* If I were a company boss, and a candidate from the same school as me came for a job, I would probably say, "what a coincidence!" and leave it at that. But in Korea, I might feel like I should give him the job.

A *yangban* from the late 18th century. Their feudal system probably helped deepen the culture of *jeong.*

THE INVISIBLE HUG

Jeong is probably a product of Korea's difficult history. For centuries, ordinary Koreans lived in villages, under the yoke of oppressive *yangban* landlords. This, and frequent crop failures, meant that people had to band together, thinking of "us" rather than "I." Added to this is Korea's status as a pawn in the power games of bigger neighbors, like China and Japan. The experience of struggling to survive as a nation bonded Koreans together in a kind of national *jeong,* in opposition to outsiders.

Jeong creates "in" and "out" groups in every situation. In the context of you and your family, the guy you went to school with is an outsider. But he becomes an insider when you meet up in Seoul. And someone from Seoul whom you never met before can share a bond with you if you encounter her in Mexico. For this reason, Koreans are famous for sticking together when abroad.

My Own Experience With *Jeong*

I experienced a kind of "nationalistic" *jeong* during my graduate school days back in England. Our class was very international, and included ten Koreans. One professor told us to submit assignments on CD-R, so I asked a Korean classmate (who I knew had a pack of ten) if I could use one of his. I had recently done a favor for him, so it wasn't unreasonable for me to ask. He declined, saying, "Ah, but we are ten." "We" meant the Korean students. He had bought the CD-Rs to share among his Korean classmates only.

The thing that frustrated me most was that this fellow told me that he was not especially friendly with half of his Korean classmates. That is part of *jeong* as well—even if you don't like someone, you can share a sense of connectedness which makes you feel the need to help them. There is even an expression, *miun jeong* ("hateful *jeong*"), to describe the *jeong* that exists between people who do not like each other. But *jeong* is beautiful too, when you enjoy such a relationship with someone. The level of self-sacrifice and mutual support shared with a good Korean friend will be very high. I have experienced the positive side of *jeong* on many occasions here—such as when I was completely broke and was able to borrow a fairly hefty amount of money from a friend, without even asking. "Just give it back when you can," I was told.

A "UNIQUELY KOREAN" EMOTION?

Sometimes, people will claim that *jeong* is something only found in Korea. In my view, this is completely false. A feeling of shared destiny, along with self-sacrifice and extreme displays of generosity, can all be found anywhere in the world. And a warm feeling towards someone, which inspires you to help them no matter what, is not a uniquely Korean emotion. But the fact that Korean has a very frequently-used word for it is telling. *Jeong* may not be "uniquely" Korean, but it is a concept to which Korean society attaches extra-strong importance.

What is *Han*?

Like *jeong*, *han* describes something that is central to the image of Korea and Koreans. *Han* is a kind of deep melancholic feeling that comes from an unresolvable burden. Perhaps you have been oppressed by someone powerful; perhaps someone close to you passed away before their time; or, perhaps the love of your life abandoned you. You cannot do anything about it, so with a heavy sense of resignation, you carry the pain around with you for the rest of your life. This is *han*.

HAN AND HEUNG

Often when Westerners think of East Asians, the stereotypes of stoicism and self-control—the so-called "inscrutable Oriental"—come to mind. But Koreans in fact tend to be very expressive and open with their feelings. Somehow, sadness and happiness both seem to be magnified in Korea. Two key cultural code-words will help us examine this further: *han* and *heung*.

HEUNG AND HAN-PULI

Because *han* comes from unresolvable trauma, its cause never goes away. So what do you do about it? You can wallow in your pain, but you can also temporarily forget about it by pursuing all-out, manic fun. This is where *heung* comes in. *Heung* is pure joy. The word isn't as famous as *han*, but I think that it should be. Even traditional Korean funerals used to feature extreme alcohol consumption, raucous singing, and the like.

Whether you want to "untie" your *han* (*han-puli*), or simply go a little crazy, Korea is a great place in which to do it. Young or old, rich or poor, everyone is allowed to get drunk, dance like a fool, or sing at the top of their voice. Tapgol Park in Seoul is often full of pensioners drinking rice wine, and throwing some shapes to the sound of old Korean music.

Korea has a history of poverty, colonialist invasion, and latterly, division into two separate countries. And crucially, a national narrative has been built around these sad events. While South Koreans can be justifiably proud of what they have achieved in such a short space of time, they still tend to view their country as a tragic victim. Korean art reflects this: the most popular ballads, TV drama series, and movies, tend to have a seriously melancholic, *han*-like aspect to them.

A traditional Korean funeral was a noisy, colorful affair full of *han-puli*.

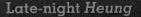

Late-night *Heung*

Korea isn't famous as a party destination—but it should be. If you find yourself out and about at 5 AM on a Friday or Saturday night, you can always drop by an "afterclub," which as its name suggests, just gets going after normal clubs are winding down. Roadside bars named *pojang macha* serve *soju*—the lethal Korean national spirit—at all hours, too. Then try a *noraebang* (a kind of karaoke room) with your friends. Thousands of English songs are also available, and even if you can't sing, there's no excuse not to dance and shake a tambourine.

MILITARY SERVICE: THE FORMATIVE YEARS

All Korean men of sound mind and body must spend two years serving as conscripted soldiers. It is a tough experience that no one looks forward to. But it is also a highly formative period in a young man's life, and one that results in life-long friendships. It also has a major influence on company life, strengthening hierarchy and unity between male co-workers.

Kim Kyung-hyup, a friend of mine, served in the marines—*haebyeongdae* in Korean. *Haebyeongdae* is considered the toughest and most tightly-knit of the services a conscript can enter. I asked him a few questions about his life then, and military service in general.

What kind of training do you go through?

Before joining a unit, you have six weeks of basic training down at Pohang [a city on the southeast coast]. Traditionally *Haebyeongdae* recruits receive training from a non-commissioned officer, a tough drill instructor who really bullies you for six weeks. In the first week they put you through tests, and send you back [to the regular army] if you aren't physically or mentally strong enough. After that, basic training proper starts—lifting tree trunks, and training in the mud. In the third week, you learn how to shoot, and something called *Bbangbbare* starts. *Bbangbbare* means waking you up in the middle of a winter's night, and forcing you to train outside wearing only your pants. Then they'll spray you with a fire hose. That's a *Haebyeongdae* tradition. It's so cold... and you can't sleep...

Bbangbbare continues, but in the fourth week you also start guerrilla and airlift training. Following that is tactical marching up Cheonjabong [a mountain around Pohang], and amphibious vehicle training. Finally, in week six, it's the completion ceremony. The whole place is a sea of tears—six weeks of built up pain and emotions just come flooding out.

What happens after that?

When you complete your six weeks you are assigned to a division, where you'll spend the rest of your two years. The main ones for *Haebyeongdae* are based in Pohang, Kimpo, and Baekryeong-do [an island very close to North Korea]. As for me, I was stationed at Baekryeong-do. Baekryeong-do *Haebyeongdae* is basically the northern-most line of defense in the West Sea. My unit was known as a special forces surprise attack unit. We differed from usual soldiers in that we did lots of training with IBS

Elite *Haebyeongdae* soldiers in training.

(Inflatable Boat, Small). This is a black rubber boat that carries seven people and weighs 230 lbs (105 kg).

What was the toughest part?

Something called "twelve kilometer head-carrying," which is a kind of training for secret landing, infiltration, and reconnaissance. Six of us would have to carry one IBS on our heads, for twelve kilometers. If you haven't done it, you can't imagine how painful it is. You really think it's going to break your spine. When you complete it and put the boat down and your seniors congratulate you, you can't help but cry. My best memories of the military were the times when I got to sit down with a beer after head-carrying. We'd receive extra money for it as well, 40,000 won each. It's more now, but at the time that was enough to enjoy yourself on a leave day.

Also, *Haebyeongdae* has a lot of idiots. For example, seniors who dig up bugs and force you to eat them. Lizards, frogs, caterpillars too. And if you have to work at night with rotten seniors, they might beat you. There was always some bastard like that.

What is the effect of military service on a young man?

You feel thankful to your parents, and also that that you helped Korean society. You lament the loss of two years of your life on rotten work, but you do become more mature.

In some ways it is cruel to spend two years conscripted into the army. Generally, Korean guys go in their second year of university, and then come back two years later. By the time they've graduated, they're about 26 or 27 years old. That's late compared to other countries. Of course, there are many who emerge more mature, but there are also a lot who think it was a waste of time.

What impact do you think military service has on Korean society?

Military service is a very important part of Korean life. Simply because we're a divided country, we have conscription, and the only people who don't go are either the physically or mentally handicapped, or those who have enough power and connections to get out of it [this is actually a highly controversial issue in Korea]. For ordinary guys,

the only choice you have is between *Haebyeongdae*, Air Force, the regular Army, and so on—there's no escape from conscription itself.

While going through the course of military service, we commonly hear that it is "character-building." But what that really means is learning socially expected behavior and rank, and being re-educated to live the kind of existence society demands us to live. The habits that form there come to last a lifetime, so military service seems to have a massive impact on how Korean men live in society.

In a good way and a bad way, conscription has a huge impact on Korean society. Not just simply as an organization for national defense, but as one of the most important elements of Korean social structure. And the *Haebyeongdae* Veterans' Association, for instance, is one of the very strongest social organizations in Korea.

Would you like to reform the system in any way?

Fundamentally, I am against conscription. We just have it because we're a divided country. I received training for two years, but really, I think that's too short a time. Conscripts don't have a strong will to protect the country, but rather, do it because they are forced to. And because there are so many soldiers, the quality of training cannot but be weakened. A professional army would be better prepared for war, because soldiers would receive proper training and live as life-long soldiers. I think that soon, we might start taking this course.

There are guys who say that women should go to the army too... but I don't think that's necessary.

KATUSA Some Korean conscripts are seconded to the US Army in a program named KATUSA. Such soldiers are considered lucky—they get to practice English, and even go home at night rather than staying in barracks.

PUTTING KOREA ON THE MAP
KOREA AS NUMBER ONE

Since the days of President Park Chung-hee, Koreans have had it drummed into them that their nation absolutely has to stack up against others, when it comes to anything that can be measured in numbers. That includes economic data, such as the value of Korean exports—but it now also extends to intellectual, cultural, and sporting fields. Whenever a Nobel prize ceremony goes by without a Korean winner, disappointed newspaper columnists churn out laments.

President Kim Dae-jung won the Nobel Peace Prize in 2000. To date, he remains Korea's only Nobel laureate.

Major sporting events result in big displays of national pride. But it's also great fun: there's no party like a World Cup party in Korea.

Korean Olympic team's medal table rank has been consistently improving, and that Psy's "Gangnam Style" hit number two in the US pop chart. In fact, "Gangnam Style" not making number one was itself a story. When will Korea have its first US Billboard number one, ran the headlines?

Psy horse-dancing. Psy became the most famous Korean ever during the summer of 2012. He is a hero to many Koreans for putting their country on the map. The government responded in kind, by putting him on a series of postage stamps.

WHY DOES KOREA NEED TO BE NUMBER ONE?

This desire to measure up is a result of Korea's troubled history. Korea is a small nation that has long been subject to the whims of larger, more powerful ones. In particular, Japanese colonization (1910–1945) created a sense of humiliation, and a desire to improve Korea's power and stature. The division of Korea into North and South heightened this. Reduced not just in terms of size and population but also in terms of power and security, both countries reacted in extreme ways.

For North Korea, that meant bulking up militarily, but for the South under Park Chung-hee, it meant pursuing economic growth. Economic performance is of course measured numerically, and Park himself was personally obsessed with Korean economic data. He would become angry at underlings who could not match his knowledge of inflation and export statistics. And over time, the national preoccupation with numbers spread into other areas of human achievement.

A surprisingly high number of Koreans know the size of national GDP, and how this stacks up against other countries. They know that Korea is the number one country in shipbuilding and semiconductors. They also know that the

Times Square
A Samsung advert in Times Square, New York. Korean businesses, campaigners, and government officials all consider New York as the prime place in which to launch any promotion. This reflects the importance of America in the South Korean psyche.

"BIG BROTHER" AMERICA

Since the division of Korea, the South has felt great political, economic, and cultural influence from "big brother" America. The land of Uncle Sam was held out to Koreans as the model *seonjinguk*—advanced nation—that they needed to emulate. Some Koreans love America, and some hate it, but nobody ignores it. This is why the US pop chart number one is the holy grail for a Korean pop star. Top Korean labels like SM Entertainment have spent millions of dollars on promoting their acts in America.

It is not inaccurate to state that Korea has a certain inferiority complex with regard to the US. This is a country that wants to be recognized, particularly by Americans. Whenever Korean activist groups want to draw attention to territorial

Korea meets America, in the Seoul district of Itaewon.

disputes with Japan, they take out adverts in *The New York Times*. It is also likely the reason why the government spent US$5 million opening a Korean restaurant in New York.

The ironic thing is though that Korea has in many ways overtaken the US. Its citizens live longer, and are healthier, better educated, less likely to be unemployed, and less likely to live in poverty. According to surveys though, Koreans are nowhere near as happy as Americans—because of their stressful, competition-filled lives.

The Latest "It" Gadget: Anipang

Trends come and go from Korea—as they do anywhere else—but they move more quickly here, thanks to neophilia, the love of the new. They also embed themselves very deeply for the brief duration of their popularity. It is hard to live in Korea and be immune to the latest "it" gadget, fashion, or slang word.

As I write, the young woman sat opposite from me in this cafe is playing a game named Anipang. Anipang is a little like the old classic Tetris, and is played on smartphones. So far I have resisted its charms, but 12 million others in this country have not. That is almost 25 percent of the Korean population. Six months previously, nobody had heard of Anipang. And I suspect that six months from now, it will be more a case of "Do you remember Anipang?"

NAEMBI GEUNSEONG: THE BOILING POINT

There is a phrase in Korean, *naembi geunseong*, which means "boiling-pot disposition." It is similar in character to the coming and going of trends like Anipang, but relates more to anger which bubbles over when heat is applied, but cools down soon afterwards. When a politician does something wrong, he has no place to hide—everyone is out to get him. But the scandal usually blows over quickly, and soon enough, he is back in frontline politics.

The summer 2008 "beef protests" illustrated *naembi geunseong* quite well, when around a million people took to the streets of Seoul in fury at the government. The demonstrations had a number of disparate causes, but the spark was undoubtedly President Lee Myung-bak's decision to reintroduce American beef imports in spite of alleged cases of mad cow disease.

By 2010, Korea was the number one importer of American beef in Asia. People eat it now without a moment's thought. And nobody protests against it.

ALL TOGETHER NOW

I write for a living. That means I inevitably spend a large part of any day alone. Unless I have a specific appointment, I'll work by myself in cafes, and have lunch by myself, too. It doesn't bother me—in fact, I rather like it.

One drawback is that I'm limited in terms of the places I can go. Korea is all about the group, so even the most casual restaurants, for instance, are set up for a minimum of two. Individual restaurant seating, as found commonly in Japan, is hard to come by. There's nothing to stop me from taking a table by myself, but it would just seem a little odd—making me look like a *wangtta* ("outcast"). What's more, most of my favorite Korean dishes, such as *dakdoritang*, a spicy chicken stew, come in big pots to be shared between three or four. You can't order an individual portion.

HAVE A GOOD EXCUSE!

During my days at a large Korean investment firm, we would have lunch all together as a team, virtually every single day of the week. At a team lunch, the most senior person would simply decide where we were going, leaving everyone else with no choice

You'll Never Walk Alone

But the don't-be-alone mindset does have some advantages. In 2005, I was working for a small investment firm in Seoul. For the first six months, my fellow new hires and I were paid like interns—receiving the princely sum of 500,000 won (around US$500) per month, an amount that barely covered my rent. But we survived, gathering virtually every day after work in each other's studio apartments, eating instant ramyeon noodles and drinking *soju*. We didn't need much money, because we lived cheaply, and we had each other's friendship. A group of eight of us spent virtually all our waking hours together. I still look back on that time as one of the happiest in my life.

Nobody wants to be alone.

over what to eat. As a so-called "individualistic" Westerner, I found this quite stifling, and often wanted a day off from it. The only way to escape was to sneak out unnoticed at 11.57 AM, and then come back an hour later, with a story about having met up with an old friend.

This kind of full-on togetherness can also cause friction in Korean-foreigner friendships. Back home, I would accept, "Sorry Dan, I'm worn out and just feel like having an afternoon in by myself watching TV," as a reason for not meeting me one particular day.

In Korea though, I would never say that to a friend. While plenty of Koreans do want to steal a moment to themselves, openly saying so may cause disappointment. So instead, I would pretend that I had something important to do.

Are You Still Single?

Being single is tough in Korea. People will ask, "Haven't you met anyone yet?" with pitying looks on their faces. Some couples proudly display their attached-ness by wearing the same outfit as each other. This is known as *couple-ot* ("couple-clothing"). If she wears a red sweater and blue jeans, so will he. And those who take each other seriously will exchange "couple rings," to show the world that they are in a relationship.

If you live in Korea and have no significant other, you may find people enjoy telling you, "I know this great guy/girl, let me introduce you to him/her." It even happens to me a lot these days. I'm glad people care about me, but I always just reply, "Don't worry about me," and tell them I'm a *nuni-nopeun saram*—a person with "high eyes," or rather, excessively high standards. I'm not sure if anyone believes that, though!

Life in the Pressure Cooker

I love Korea, and I love living in Korea. But I do sometimes feel grateful to be an outsider here. The reason for this is the perpetual competition. This country has a pressure-cooker environment in which winners and losers are identified from an early age. It starts with education—along with money, the most important element of a person's social status in Korea—and then moves on to career and marriage. The birth of children then marks the beginning of a new cycle of competition.

This competition mania kicked off in the 1960s, when President Park Chung-hee exhorted the people to go all-out for industrial development. As a nation, South Korea was compelled to hit ever-higher export figures and GDP targets, to overtake North Korea and other countries. Korea had no natural resources to speak of, so everything rested on the optimal use of brains and brawn. This required absolute devotion to academic study, and then absolute devotion to work after graduation.

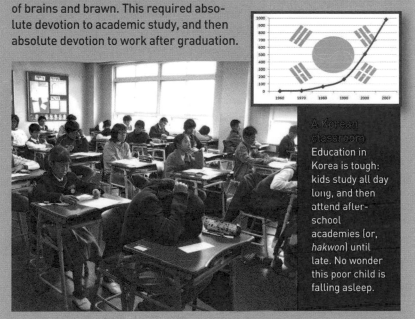

A Korean classroom Education in Korea is tough: kids study all day long, and then attend after-school academies (or, *hakwon*) until late. No wonder this poor child is falling asleep.

THE EARLY REWARDS OF COMPETITION

Those who did well—going to the best universities and then working for the best companies, or taking up government service—were rewarded amply. Through their herculean efforts, they rose as Korea rose. They enjoyed elevated social status and wealth. Lee Myung-bak, for instance, collected refuse from the streets to pay his tuition fees at the elite Korea University, and later joined Hyundai Engineering and Construction. An early employee with an extreme capacity for hard work, he became CEO in his thirties, and was later lionized in a TV drama series about his life. In 2007, he was elected president.

Now-former President Lee was an archetype of late 20th century Korean achievement. His personal success is a kind of model—get into an elite university, join a good company, work like crazy, and push your way to the top. Naturally, this is a decent route to take in any country, but in Korea, it is treated as just about the only route. If you stray from this golden path, you are made to feel like you failed.

"SPEC"—A MODERN CULTURAL CODEWORD

These days, 80 percent of young people go to university, with 500,000 university graduates coming on to the job market every year. Unfortunately, high-status companies and government agencies can only create around 100,000 jobs in that time. Because of the importance of being seen to be doing well, people are reluctant to take jobs with less famous organizations, or engage in blue collar work. If they did so, their later marriage prospects and social position would be greatly weakened—so they wait, and build up their resumes.

A person with a resume stuffed full of impressive qualifications is said to have "spec." Spec can mean Masters and PhD degrees, as well as professional qualifications such as the Certified Financial Analyst (CFA) certification. In other countries, people already working in finance take the CFA, but in Korea, university students feel compelled to do so. Many Korean ex-co-workers of mine

had at least the Level One CFA before they even set foot in the office.

It is also considered essential to ace English tests like the TOEIC and TOEFL. People even spend years living abroad to better their chances at doing so, but actual fluency itself is not so important. The exam result is everything, as it is one of the main means by which large companies whittle down their applicant lists.

All work and no play makes Jack a dull boy, of course. There are many young people in Korea with virtually no time for hobbies or travel, because of the perceived need to build spec. One of my best friends is like this. It isn't that he likes that lifestyle, but rather, he always felt that he needed to concentrate on developing his marketability to survive in this hyper-competitive society.

The fruits of one's labor...

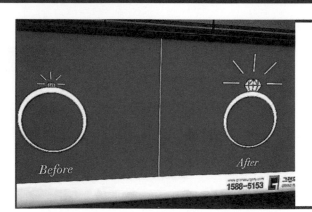

Top Talent, a competition show for English-speaking performers. English fluency is one of the main ways in which Korean society divides people into winners and losers. Those who can speak English very well are admired and respected for it.

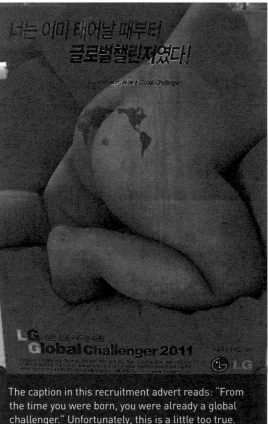

너는 이미 태어날 때부터 글로벌챌린저였다!

(You were born to be a Global Challenger!)

LG Global Challenger 2011　LG

The caption in this recruitment advert reads: "From the time you were born, you were already a global challenger." Unfortunately, this is a little too true.

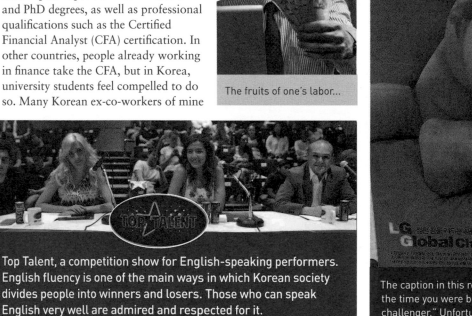

Before　After

1588-5153

Plastic Surgery to Get Ahead?

An advert for plastic surgery. The message is, "Be a more competitive potential wife, and get a richer husband." But a pretty face can also get you a better job. At one company I worked for, female candidates were regularly screened based on the attractiveness of the mandatory photograph affixed to the application form. There is even an expression, *Chwijik seonghyung* ("surgery for getting a job"). Don't label a Korean woman as vain for going under the knife: she may even consider surgery necessary for her career.

Above The North Face (see "Always In Stokke," right) is a very popular brand in Korea. But have you heard of this cheaper imitator, The Red Face? Below Samsung headquarters (on the right), Gangnam, Seoul. There are many who dream of the chance of working here.

THE COMPETITION NEVER ENDS

Congratulations! You've spent your life building up great spec, and finally, you have a job with XYZ *Chaebol*. But your life will still be stressful, as you will work extremely long hours (the longest in the OECD), and you will still be competing for promotions at the office. Unless you are a superstar, you will be pushed out for early retirement around the age of fifty, to face an uncertain future. So in order to prolong your career as much as possible, you must continue fighting all the way. And meanwhile, your children will be under great pressure to come top of their class.

Recently, the phrase "Scandi-Mom" has done the rounds in the Korean media. This refers to a mother who pursues an apparently "Scandinavian" style of parenting—reducing pressure on her kids, and encouraging them to play more. There are also young people who are deliberately dropping out of the success track. I have several highly intelligent friends who are completely uninterested in spec, getting a job at Samsung, or even in getting married. But both they and the Scandi-Mom are very much in the minority. Competition will remain the defining characteristic of modern Korea for the foreseeable future.

Always in *Stokke*

Particularly for those of high social status, it is important to always be seen to be doing well. This is a big part of the reason why Korea spends five percent of GDP on luxury brands, higher than any other country. One of the more interesting trends in luxury over the past few years has been the explosive growth in popularity of Stokke baby strollers. Stokke strollers are imported from Norway, and despite performing no better than other strollers in consumer tests, their US$700–1500 price tag makes them, paradoxically, a must-have item for Gangnam mothers. All of the guys at the investment firm I used to work at have become fathers, and most of them have had to cough up for a Stokke.

In 2013, a Korean firm went one step further and even bought Stokke itself! Among teenage boys, jackets by The North Face are beyond fashionable—even though they are more expensive in Korea than in other countries. It is common to see groups of youths walking along, all wearing the same type of North Face jacket. Costly threads are important—but in a group-oriented society, there is also a demand to not stand out too much.

Your Phone Disgusts Me!

I finally caved in and bought a smartphone in December 2011. For a long time, I was alone among my friends in resisting the trend. This often exposed me to mockery. One day, I was sitting in a cafe, with my stone-age phone out on the table in front of me. A mother and her son (of about seven or eight years old) walked past, and the boy blurted out, "Ahh, *yetnal* phone! Hahaha!" (*yetnal* means "old"). He was pointing at the thing, and had a look of total disgust on his face. Yet only two years previously, my phone had been the "latest" thing!

A CLASH OF OLD AND NEW

Korea was one of the "Asian Tiger" economies, experiencing extremely impressive economic growth throughout most of the late 20th century. The driving force behind this was authoritarian President Park Chung-hee, who saw industrial development as the country's way out of poverty. It was also a way of overcoming the sense of shame and weakness felt because of Japanese colonialism, and a means of gaining security against the threat of North Korea.

Everything related to the past had to go. Old was bad, even shameful. Thatched roofs were out and corrugated sheet metal was in as part of President Park's "New Village Movement" (*Saemaeul Undong*) in the 1970s; *hanoks*—traditional Korean houses—were torn down and replaced with gigantic gray apartment complexes. Then when the apartment complexes started to get old, they were torn down and replaced with newer apartment complexes.

The spirit of those times still exists. Koreans tend to like anything new and exciting. Slang vocabulary changes all the time. Restaurants last for two or three years, before their owners close them down and start serving something different. A hit from last year is an "old" song.

THE NEW NOSTALGIA

Neophilia has become a default cultural setting. But the pace of change is now slowing, and people have enough in the way of material comforts. This means that it is becoming easier to look back wistfully on the past. Normally I wouldn't consider nostalgia an especially good thing, but in the case of Korea, I think it is. The fact that *hanoks* are making a comeback, along with other traditional elements of Korean heritage (see next chapter), means that Koreans are getting over the sense of embarrassment they had of their history, and re-learning their love for the best aspects of the past.

It is absolutely not contradictory to own a modernized *hanok*, fit it up with lightning-speed broadband, and hang old *minhwa* paintings on its walls. In fact, you would have to be quite wealthy to do so, and people would admire your taste. It is in fact the social elite who are leading the nostalgia boom. Where the traditional was once cheap, it is now expensive. *Hanoks* in the Seoul district of Bukchon could have been snapped up for the low tens of thousands of dollars a few years back; today, some go for millions. A haute couture traditional *hanbok* dress can cost thousands.

A *hanok* in Bukchon. Just a few years ago, people thought *hanoks* were old-fashioned. Today, modernized versions like these are highly sought after.

Musical Nostalgia

There is also nostalgia for music. Bars and clubs which exclusively play old Korean pop from the 60s and 70s are springing up. Shin Joong-hyun, the most legendary Korean rock star, told me that back in the 1980s, he was considered old news. Now, in his late 70s, he is playing again in big concert halls. Younger musicians, particularly in the Hongdae art school district of Seoul, speak of him with absolute reverence.

Those who are interested in old-school Korean rock should go to the funky Gopchang Jeongol bar in Hongdae, which has literally thousands of old vinyl records. At weekends, you'll have to wait a while to get a table. But it is worth it—the crowd there is friendly, and you'll invariably end up meeting artists, writers, and other interesting characters. And the age range goes from about 20 to 60.

At the moment, the mainstream is still driven forward by neophilia, whilst nostalgia is the preserve of the wealthy and the arty. But trends usually start with those latter two groups. In the next ten or twenty years, I think we'll start seeing mass construction of *hanoks* again, and a boom in old Korean rock memorabilia. I'm definitely keeping hold of my signed Shin Joong-hyun CD.

LOVE AND COURTSHIP IN KOREA: DATING AND MARRIAGE, KOREAN-STYLE

Korean weddings tend to be big and expensive—the bigger and more expensive, the better. I have seen Korean wedding cakes as tall as myself, and heard of bills of ten thousand dollars just for flowers. I have been to weddings where five hundred people showed up, and guests arrived by the coachload.

Why is this? In Korea, a wedding is not just a union between two people. It is one of two families tying their fortunes together. The groom's father's co-workers, many of whom the groom himself will not really know, will likely show up. The bride's aunt's friends may come along to offer congratulations. And naturally, both families want to put on a good show. A big wedding is a matter of pride.

A MARRIAGE MONEY-GO-ROUND

A clever family might not end up out of pocket on their son or daughter's wedding, though. This is because guests give the highly practical gift of cash in an envelope. When you arrive at a Korean wedding, you will see two tables—one manned by friends of the groom, and one by friends of the bride. You sign a book of congratulation, and then they hand you an envelope, into which you may put 50,000 or 100,000 won—maybe more, if you are close (or rich).

All of those contributions should hopefully pay for the lavish wedding meal (and copious amounts of alcohol), flowers, room hire, dresses, and so on. Some families even turn a profit. But because the money goes to the family rather than the bride and groom themselves, some guests—usually the groom's friends—hand extra cash over to them in secret.

Between the two families, a whole range of expensive gifts will also change hands. The groom's family is supposed to provide an apartment for the couple, while the bride's family is supposed to fill it with furniture, appliances, and so on. The bride must in turn give the groom's family a gift, or *yedan*, which consists of valuables up to the tune of 10 percent of the cost of the apartment! Many a wedding has been called off due to disputes over these costly arrangements.

A wedding at the Ritz-Carlton Hotel in Gangnam. This was one of the fanciest weddings I have ever attended. Check out the size of the cake in the background!

The mothers of both bride and groom at a wedding. A Korean wedding is a union of families rather than just individuals—so the two sides really need to get along.

Don't Marry Her!

Because a Korean wedding is a union of families, parents are heavily involved even in the selection process. Even today, most Koreans would not defy their parents if told "don't marry him/her." A close friend of mine broke up with his girlfriend after his parents said they could not accept her as a daughter-in-law. He later married another woman. Sad to say, the difference was one of status—his mother and father felt the family of the first girlfriend to be socially beneath them. This kind of tale is a common one in Korea.

EOJANG GWALLI: MANAGING YOUR FISHING GROUNDS

My aforementioned friend met both his ex-girlfriend and future wife on blind dates. These are known in Korea as *sogaeting*. *Sogaeting* is considered the standard way of meeting people, and it certainly isn't merely the desperate who have them. Many people also enjoy arranging them. Internet dating, too, is popular, with relatively little stigma attached. And then for more serious dating, there are "marriage information" agencies, which introduce people looking for a spouse. Large firms like Duo and Sunoo, which maintain databases of tens of thousands of lonely hearts, do great business.

In big cities like Seoul though, there are many who do their own "hunting" (this is an English loan-word), at their universities, in bars, and in clubs, and so on. And despite Korea's (now outdated) reputation for social conservatism, those who are considered attractive may well maintain a pool of not-quite-significant others whom they date casually and non-exclusively, before possibly getting serious with one of them later. Young Koreans even came up with a phrase, *eojang gwalli* ("managing your fishing grounds"), to describe this practice.

A *Sogaeting* (Blind Date)

Blind dates are the most common kind of first date in Korea. Mutual friends introduce the two, and then leave them to it. Sometimes things work out, and sometimes they don't...

YOU'RE MY PET!

Another interesting trend has been the growth in relationships between older women and younger men. "Nunaism"—"*nuna*" being "older sister," but which can also generally mean an older woman—has gained traction in art and life. TV shows and movies show such relationships, and this has been accompanied by a dramatic increase in the number of men marrying older women in the past fifteen years. This is helping turn the traditional man-as-provider notion on its head. There was even a movie released in 2011 entitled *You're My Pet*, in which a career woman protagonist finds a poor young man on the street, and quite literally takes him in as her pet. The male lead is Jang Keun-seok, an archetypal pretty-boy (or *kkotminam* in Korean slang) who is also extremely popular in Japan.

The Man of Korea Movement:
You're My Pet enraged a group named Man of Korea (MoK), a self-proclaimed men's rights organization, which protests against submissive portrayals of men in the media. MoK also threw a hissy fit about a pop video by singer Baek Ji-young, which showed men being treated like pet dogs by women.

It is surprising that such a group would exist in a country as male-dominated as Korea, but it does show that times are starting to change. Ironically, the media companies that release Miss Baek's songs, and make movies like *You're My Pet*, are still almost completely run by men.

THE *AEGYO* SYNDROME: GIRLINESS TO THE MAX

"Am I cute?"
"Sure, you're cute."

"But then, am I not pretty?"
"Yes, of course you're pretty."

"Why don't you say I'm sexy, though?"
"You just asked me if you're pretty..."

"So I'm not sexy then?"
"I didn't say that! Sure you are."

"But if I'm sexy, then how can I be cute?"
"'Cute' and 'sexy' are different."

[Repeat until one's head explodes]

This is a close approximation of a conversation I once had with a girl I was dating, back when I was young and foolish. But this kind of rather childish, overly-cute talk is an example of *aegyo*, a type of girlish flirtiness that young Korean women are adept at. Though it may frustrate a cynical Englishman like me, the truth is that plenty of Korean guys go crazy for it.

HOW *AEGYO* WORKS

Basically, *aegyo* is all about seeming as cute or defenseless as possible, whilst teasing the man a little. Squealing the word "*oppa*"—which literally means "older brother" but is mostly used to address a boyfriend—is a must. So is comically slapping *oppa* on the chest or arm whenever he says anything a bit naughty. Pouting and pretending to be angry for a while, and then forgiving *oppa*, also increases one's *aegyo* rating.

The master *aegyo* artist is a completely different woman in front of a man she is interested in. She may use bad language, discuss all manner of sexual topics, and drink like a fish when with her female friends, but if the object of her affections shows up, the change is instantaneous. She will become a picture of giggly innocence.

AEGYO OR *NAESUNG*?

Not everyone likes *aegyo*. For a start, women tend to hate it when they see others using it—though that doesn't necessarily stop them using *aegyo* themselves when required. There is also the occasional man who finds it irritating, particularly when he is not attracted to the woman in question. In such a case, he might accuse her of being *naesung*, rather than having *aegyo*. *Naesung* means "pretending to be innocent," but in a negative way.

Feminists tend to dislike *aegyo*, since it reinforces the "helpless woman" stereotype, and encourages men to see women in that light. But one can also see *aegyo* as a kind of empowering con game that induces men to become putty in a cute young lady's manicured hands. And I have seen women with fat salaries and PhDs demonstrate *naesung* with the best of them.

Is she really angry, or is she just using *aegyo*?

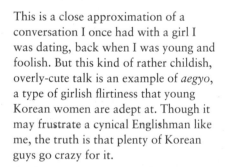

Aegyo makes great business

Korean girl groups like Girls' Generation and f(x) have young (i.e. teenage) members who are trained how to use their *aegyo* to maximum effect when appearing in videos and interviews. At the same time, they also dress in an extremely sexualized fashion. Apparently, the fans who really like this are older men in their late thirties or forties, some of whom even send gifts and fan mail to their favorite group members. It is hard to deny that there is something a little not-quite-right about this. But it is very good business for the record labels.

PART 2

TRADITIONAL
KOREA

Before we rush headlong into K-pop or the sometimes scary world of the "netizen," let's look at some of the foundations of Korean culture. I'm talking about the likes of religion and ethics, traditional arts, and the classic Korean house. But don't run away just yet—these are also subjects that take in shamanistic fortune-telling and flying Taekwondo kicks. As I said, Korea will never bore you.

CRITICAL EVENTS IN KOREAN HISTORY

GOJOSEON, THE FIRST "PROTO-KOREAN" STATE

The first identifiably Korean state was Gojoseon, the territory of which covers much of modern-day Manchuria and North Korea. Its foundation is shrouded in mystery. The 2333 BC figure is merely a guess based on readings of the tale of Dangun, the legendary "first Korean." The story begins with Hwanin, the "Lord of Heaven," sending his son Hwanung to live on earth. Hwanung arrived at Cheonji (Heaven Lake) on top of Baekdusan, the tallest and most spiritually important mountain on the Korean peninsula. Hwanung heard the prayers of a tiger and a bear who wanted to become human. He told them that if they stayed in a cave for a hundred days, eating only mugwort and garlic, he would grant their wish. The tiger gave up, but the bear persevered and was transformed into a woman. She later prayed for a husband, and Hwanung himself took her as his wife. Their son, Dangun, became the mythical founder of Gojoseon, a state which lasted until the first century BC.

Na Cheol (1863–1916) founded Daejonggyo, a religion that worships Dangun.

KOREA FIRST UNIFIED, 668 AD

From the first to the seventh centuries AD, what would today be called "Korea" was in fact three separate states—Goguryeo, Baekje, and Silla. Silla conquered Baekje in 660, and eight years later, claimed Goguryeo. This came with the eventual loss of Goguryeo's northern territory— some Korean historians lament this downsizing of Korea even today. Regardless, 668 is the year in which we can say "Korea" truly began.

Left A Silla crown. **Above** Cheomseongdae observatory at Gyeongju, the capital of Silla.

Gyeongbokgung, the main palace of the Joseon Dynasty. Gyeongbokgung remains the most well-known Korean palace.

1392—The Joseon Dynasty

Four centuries of Koryo and the cracks were showing. Mongol invasions had weakened the state, and powerful monks were taking advantage of Buddhism's status as the national religion to accumulate vast wealth. Supported by anti-Buddhist, neo-Confucianist hardliners, General Yi Seong-gye established himself as king of the new Joseon Dynasty in 1392, four years after taking de facto control in a coup.

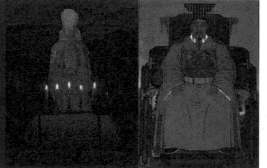

Right Koryo Dynasty-era Buddha statue at Gaesong, in present-day North Korea. Gaesong was the capital of Korea back then. Seoul only became capital in 1394, at the beginning of the Joseon Dynasty. Far right Wang Geon.

King Sejong the Great, the most revered ruler of the Joseon era. He reigned from 1418–1450 and presided over the creation of Hangeul, the Korean writing system.

세종대왕

THE KORYO DYNASTY

By the early 900s, Korea had again split into three separate states. One of those was Hugoguryeo (later Goguryeo), which was led by Gung Ye—a man known for his brutality and rather mad behavior (he killed his own wife and children, and declared himself a Buddha). His prime minister Wang Geon overthrew him, and succeeded in reuniting the whole of Korea in 936. Wang Geon's new kingdom took the name Koryo. If you ever wondered where the word "Korea" comes from, there's your answer.

THE IMJIN WAE-RAN INVASIONS

For a period of six years, Japanese invaders attempted to take control of Korea. They failed thanks to Admiral Yi Sun-sin's astonishing naval prowess. He won a famous victory at the 1597 Battle of Myeongnyang, despite being outnumbered 333 ships to 13—and the assistance of Chinese troops. But Korea's survival came at the cost of hundreds of thousands of lives. Imjin Wae-ran also represents the start of Korea's obsession with spicy red pepper: the Japanese brought it over with them, having obtained it from Portuguese traders.

JAPANESE COLONIZATION

Joseon had been seriously weakened by infighting and corruption, unfortunately making Japan's next major attempt at taking control of Korea easier. Korea became a "protectorate" in 1910, and was used as a staging post by Japan in which to invade China. Koreans were forced to take Japanese names, and many women were even made into sex slaves. Liberation came in 1945, with the fall of Imperial Japan to the Allies, but the 35 years of Japanese rule continues to cast a long shadow over Korea: the period created both heroes and collaborators, and political divisions that last to this day.

1950–1953—The Korean War

Following liberation, two Korean states emerged—each backed by a superpower. North Korean leader Kim Il-sung was personally chosen by the Soviets, and the South had Lee Seung-man (Syngman Rhee), a Harvard-educated Methodist whom the Americans trusted (well, at least initially). Both wanted to reunify the country under their sole command, and after a series of skirmishes, the North launched a full-scale attack on June 25, 1950. The war lasted three years, claimed millions of lives, and had no victor. *From now on, our story just deals with South Korea…*

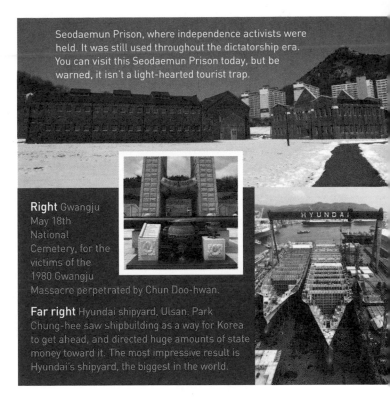

Seodaemun Prison, where independence activists were held. It was still used throughout the dictatorship era. You can visit this Seodaemun Prison today, but be warned, it isn't a light-hearted tourist trap.

Right Gwangju May 18th National Cemetery, for the victims of the 1980 Gwangju Massacre perpetrated by Chun Doo-hwan.

Far right Hyundai shipyard, Ulsan. Park Chung-hee saw shipbuilding as a way for Korea to get ahead, and directed huge amounts of state money toward it. The most impressive result is Hyundai's shipyard, the biggest in the world.

PARK CHUNG-HEE TAKES CHARGE

Army General Park Chung-hee took power in a coup on May 16, 1961. He ran a repressive regime—but one that pulled the country out of poverty and laid the foundations for South Korea's "economic miracle." He was eventually assassinated by his intelligence chief in 1979. Park Chung-hee is a controversial figure, but South Korea is in many ways still his country. His daughter, Park Geun-hye, was elected president in December 2012.

DEMOCRACY COMES TO KOREA

South Korea is home to two miracles—one economic, one political. Massive protests forced military dictator Chun Doo-hwan (who had taken over following Park's assassination) to declare free elections in 1987. Since then, a new president has been elected every five years. Newly democratic, economic powerhouse South Korea turned the 1988 Olympics into a gigantic "coming out party" to mark the nation's emergence onto the world stage.

Below North Korean refugees aboard a US Navy vessel, 1952.

The Olympic Torch, 1988

KOREA'S MULTIFACETED BELIEF SYSTEMS

For a country forever being labeled "homogeneous," there is a surprising amount of religious diversity in South Korea. It may surprise you to know that the most popular religion now is Christianity, but Buddhism and even traditional shamanism still both have many adherents. Buddhism and shamanism even blend into each other, to a large extent. And some shamanists even follow Jesus Christ. To add to this mix, Christianity itself—a Western import—has been "Koreanized" in many ways. To talk about belief systems in Korea though, we cannot ignore Confucianism. As we shall see, Confucianism is not actually a religion. But what is it? Read on and find out...

Myeongryundang, at the present-day site of Sunkyunkwan University in Seoul. Myeongryundang served as the nation's top Confucian college during the Koryo and Joseon Dynasties.

THE ENDURING INFLUENCE OF CONFUCIANISM IN KOREA

Especially after the inception of the Joseon Dynasty in 1392, Confucianism came to have great influence on Korean culture. This system of moral philosophy is an import though, having originated from the teachings of Confucius (Gong Fuzi), in ancient China. Confucianism is not a religion like Buddhism, but it does offer guidance on how people should live. Particularly, it is concerned with how people behave in relation to each other, in order to promote a harmonious society.

In a Confucian society, one must uphold certain obligations: the practice of *ren*, the humane treatment of others; *li*, the correct observance of important social rituals, such as funerals, or even the preparation of tea; and *xiao*, or filial piety. The last was the most important of all. The worst kind of person was the one who did not show sufficient respect to his or her parents.

HIGHER OR LOWER?

Confucianism is very hierarchical. Though the king had to treat his subjects humanely (because of *ren*), the people were to respond in kind with absolute subservience. All human relationships were considered to have a higher and lower partner: ruler and subject; father and son; brother and younger brother; man and wife; and, friend and friend. Equality only existed in the very last one of the five. As a result, men came to be treated as superior to women, and the old as above the young. The ideal Joseon woman was simply a "good wife and wise mother," who did not concern herself with the world outside the family home; even today, Korea's gender pay gap is the highest in the OECD.

AGE HIERARCHY

Because of Confucianism, one is expected to use a respectful form of language (known as *jondaetmal*) to those older than oneself. People even give each other titles based on their age difference: older and younger members of the same school or university are known as *seonbae* and *hubae* respectively. The *seonbae* is supposed to look out for his *hubae*, and pay for everything whenever they get together for a meal or a drink. The *hubae* ought to follow the *seonbae*'s words of guidance, and even do favors for him if requested.

Age is also a major factor in promotions in the workplace. At a typical Korean company, even the utterly brilliant must peer up from the lower rungs of the ladder for many years. But things are worse for the less-than-brilliant fifty-year-old. It would be strange for such an older "salaryman" to remain a middle manager, as younger staff would overtake him. His fat salary—which naturally increased every year in accordance with his age-derived status—is also a burden to the company. Therefore, he is pushed into early retirement. Thus Korea is full of fifty- and sixty-something men scraping a living driving taxis or working as security guards.

Left Shin Saimdang, the ideal Confucian "good wife and wise mother." She devoted herself to raising her son, the noted scholar Yulgok.

EDUCATION IN KOREA
SHUT UP AND STUDY!

The Daechi-dong neighborhood in Gangnam, Seoul, is a kind of ground zero for Korean education mania. Due to government efforts to develop Gangnam in the 1970s and 1980s, there are an abundance of good schools in the area. This resulted in spiralling property prices, and the creation of a nouveau riche elite. In turn, this drew in large numbers of private after-school academies (or *hakwon*), which can charge top dollar for extra-curricular tuition. Today, one of the main streets through Daechi-dong is known as "*hakwon* alley."

Below and right Young children learning English at a *hakwon*—a private after-school academy.

Daechi-dong kids are lucky by any material standards. They wear expensive brand name clothes, and have a great chance at entering top universities and getting top jobs later in life. They also stand to inherit million-dollar apartments. Yet, it is unlikely many of them feel fortunate. When I first lived in Seoul, I gave one lesson per week at an English *hakwon* there, and saw how extreme their education-obsessed mothers could be.

It was really not unusual to see children crying from stress. Nothing less than an "A" ever seemed to be good enough, and I heard comments like, "I went to bed at midnight after studying, and got up at 6 AM to start studying again" on a very regular basis. Korean society values education to an astonishing extent, so parents put great pressure on their children to achieve. And particularly in areas like Daechi-dong, mothers engage in vicarious competition with each other: "Our Soo-min just got into Seoul National University" will be followed with, "well, our Jae-won just got into Harvard!"

A DOUBLE-EDGED SWORD

No doubt education mania has had very positive effects on Korea—having a highly-qualified populace has contributed greatly to economic growth. However, there are great costs involved, too. The Institute for Social Development Studies at Yonsei University has found Korean teenagers to be the unhappiest in the OECD. Another study, by the Korean Educational Development Institute, also found Korean youths to be the second worst at social interaction among 36 countries surveyed.

Tragically, suicide is the leading cause of death among Korean youths. And according to Statistics Korea, 53 percent of young Koreans who have suicidal thoughts do so because of worries about education-related competition. Every year, there are many cases of high school students taking their own lives around the time of the university entrance exam.

English *hakwons* remain a great way to make money if done right. Several people have approached me asking me to open one with them, even offering to put up all the capital. But although I know I'll never change this extreme education culture—it is as Korean as *kimchi*—I don't want to be part of it.

CONFUCIANISM AND EDUCATION

One other important area where Confucianism affects Korea is education. A traditional Confucian society was supposed to be ruled by those who mastered *li*, and the way of demonstrating this was through examinations. In government-set tests, scholars had to show supreme knowledge of classic Confucian texts, ceremonies, and ethics. Those who did sufficiently well could become civil servants. In early Joseon Korea, this was virtually the only route to wealth and status. Thus the Korean education fetish was born. This country has the world's highest university enrolment rate. Even children as young as ten spend hours every day in private cram schools, which operate after regular school hours. The aim is to gain entrance into one of the "SKY" universities: Seoul National, Korea, or Yonsei University.

Black Buddhist stone piles. Each stone represents a prayer of the person who built the pile. Such features are very common around temples both in Korea and throughout the Buddhist world.

KOREAN BUDDHISM
A SHOCKED KING CONVERTS HIS KINGDOM

Buddhism first came to the Korean peninsula via a Chinese monk named Sundo, in 372 AD. In those days, there was no "unified" Korea, but rather three separate states—Goguryeo, Baekje, and Silla. The royal families of the first two came to adopt Buddhism, while their subjects mostly stuck with shamanism. Importantly though, this was never the cause of any friction. Even today, shamanism and Buddhism "blend" in Korea, meaning that those who follow one tend to follow the other as well.

BUDDHISM AS STATE RELIGION

Silla's rulers first rejected the new faith, but eventually made it into their state religion due to the actions of one man—according to legend, at least. In 527, a court official named Ichadon announced that he was a Buddhist, and implored King Beopheung to make Silla a Buddhist state. When this request was rejected, he forced his own execution by deliberately insulting members of the court. The story goes that when his head was cut off, the blood that flowed out was white, not red. Ichadon had predicted this earlier. The stunned king then converted Silla to Buddhism.

Silla unified Korea, and thus, Buddhism came to be the official religion

Apprentice monks. These young boys have had their heads shaved, in preparation for training to become monks.

of the whole peninsula. And following the fall of Silla and the proclamation of the Koryo kingdom (from which the English word "Korea" was derived) in 918, Buddhism's power grew even stronger. Lavish temples were built, and many had their own private armies. Monks were exempt from taxation. There were also extraordinary achievements: the carving of the entire Buddhist canon on to 81,258 wooden blocks, completed in 1259.

DECLINE AND RECOVERY

The founding of the Joseon Dynasty in 1392 brought in a new Confucian elite. They despised Buddhism, and like the shamanists, the once-privileged monks were pushed to the margins of society. There, Buddhism and shamanism—

Lanterns placed in honor of Buddha's birthday. In Korea, Buddha's birthday is celebrated on the eighth day of the fourth month of the lunar calendar.

A part of the *Tripitaka Koreana*, at Haeinsa temple.

Monks Behaving Badly?

There is no real "rock star CEO" in Korea. Sometimes, entire teams behave as though they were rock stars. In 2012, a major scandal tarnished the leadership of the Jogye Order, an organization which accounts for 90 percent of Korea's Buddhists, and has an annual budget of 30 billion won (around US$27 million). It emerged that senior monks were gambling, drinking, smoking, and even visiting "room salons" (hostess bars), with temple donors' money.

which had never had a hostile relationship—began to blend more closely. Even today, one can see portraits of Sanshin, the shaman mountain god, at Buddhist temples. People who seek the advice of *mudang* (shamans) will also follow the Buddha. And also like shamanism, Buddhism has undergone something of a renaissance in modern Korea. Around 23 percent of the population is Buddhist. There are popular monks who give public lectures, write bestselling books, and go on television.

BUDDHISM AND BUSINESS

And this religion, which encourages followers to group together in a "Sangha" community dedicated to sustained, mutual improvement, influences both Korean and Japanese business culture. The Japanese word *kaizen* is much-loved by management theorists, and is most frequently associated with Japanese companies like Toyota. However, its meaning—"continuous improvement"—is also applicable to Korean firms, such as Samsung Electronics. The top Korean firms operate like tight communities of dedicated team-workers, and do not tend to create radically inventive products, but rather refine and perfect existing ones. The CEO is top dog, but he is not seen as an indispensable individual, like in the US, but rather as the leader of a great team.

Buddhist temple art at Bulguksa, Gyeongju. Such *Taenghwa* art is one of the best reasons to visit a Buddhist temple in Korea, and Bulguksa is no exception.

The temple of Yonggungsa at Gijang, near Busan. Yonggungsa's location—cut into the rocky coastline—makes it one of the most visually striking temples in the whole of Korea.

CHRISTIANITY IN KOREA: THE POWERFUL NEWCOMER

Though this Western religious import has been around for several centuries, it was only in the mid and late 20th century that Christianity really began to grow rapidly. It may surprise you to learn that Christianity is now the most common faith in Korea. With the exception of East Timor, it is the country with the highest proportion of churchgoers in Asia. Korea is also second only to the US in the export of Christian missionaries.

CATHOLIC INROADS

Catholicism began to make inroads into Korea in the 17th and 18th centuries. Korean scholars based in China began studying Catholic texts, and bringing them back to their homeland. Prominent figures like scholar and reformer Dasan Jeong Yak-yong were among those who began deeply studying the incoming religion.

Myeongdong Cathedral Completed in May 1898, Myeongdong Cathedral is the center of Korean Catholicism. The cathedral was also a focal point for pro-democracy protestors in the 1970s and 1980s, with figures like Cardinal Kim Sou-hwan offering them protection there from the authorities.

Nuns enjoy a picnic in the grounds of a palace.

In 1801, the court of Queen Jeongsun grew especially fearful of Catholicism following the discovery of a letter to the Bishop of Beijing from Hwang Sa-yeong (Dasan's brother-in-law) inviting foreign powers to invade Korea. The Queen denounced Catholics as traitors, and launched the so-called Sinyu Persecution, which led to mass executions of believers.

As a result, the growth of Catholicism was impeded; by 1882, there were still only 12,500 Catholics in the whole country. Sinyu and subsequent persecutions also led Catholicism to take on an insular, quiet orientation in Korea. Even in these days of religious freedom, Korean Catholics are nowhere near as vocal about their faith as Korean Protestants.

A Protestant preacher in Myeongdong, Seoul. Usually the message of such street preachers is "repent or go to hell."

PROTESTANTISM, A SUCCESS STORY

Protestantism has had a shorter, and more successful history on the Korean peninsula. Following the opening up of Korea in the late 19th century, American missionaries like Horace Underwood and Henry Appenzeller began to arrive. They established schools, universities, and hospitals, providing Protestantism with a benevolent, progressive image.

Lee Seung-man (Syngman Rhee), the first president of the Republic of Korea, seen here embracing General Douglas MacArthur. The Rhee era was a key factor in the growth of Protestantism in Korea.

Korean Megachurches

Koreans show a tendency towards large group activity, and one result of this is the development of megachurches. Yoido Full Gospel Church in Seoul operates like a franchise, with affiliate churches all over the country. In this way, Yoido claims over a million members; another, the powerful Somang Church, has around 700,000. Unfortunately, the amount of money these churches have can create illegal incentives: family members of Yoido Church founder David Cho Yong-gi have faced trial for financial misdealing.

Protestants also played a leading role in resisting Japanese colonial rule (1910–1945). Sixteen of the thirty-three signatories of the March 1st Independence Declaration were Protestant, though only two percent of the total population followed the faith at the time.

Following the division of the peninsula, South Korea came to be strongly influenced by the United States. Americanophile Syngman Rhee—the South's first president—was a Methodist, and almost half of his government was Christian. The US became a model for Korea to emulate, and its religion was no exception in that regard. There were just 800,000 Korean Protestants in 1958, but two million ten years later; there are 11 million now. Catholicism did not grow as rapidly, but it did also increase its presence: they number around three million today.

FERVENCY AND POLITICKING

Christianity in Korea—particularly Protestantism—can polarize opinion. Korean Protestants tend to be fervent and vocal about their religion, with preachers sometimes haranguing passers-by on the street. It is also very common for them to approach foreigners, asking "Do you know Jesus Christ?" When visiting Korea, do not be surprised if complete strangers come up to you and ask you to go to their church.

Yoido Full Gospel Church by night.

Furthermore, some churches have a very aggressive political slant (generally right-wing). Prior to the 2011 Seoul mayoral election, one prominent pastor publicly announced that left-of-center candidate Park Won-soon (who eventually won) "belongs to demons and Satan." Conservative President Lee Myung-bak won election in 2007 partly due to the Protestant bloc vote.

Above Seoul Mayor Park Won-soon

KOREAN SHAMANISM
THOUSANDS OF GODS, THOUSANDS OF YEARS

Shamanism, or *musok*, is an indigenous set of folk practices based on an understanding that there exists a metaphysical realm of spirits alongside the natural world. Those spirits lie not just in people, but also in animals, trees, mountains, rivers, and rocks.

For around 40,000 years—much longer than the idea of "Korea" itself has existed—*mudang* have intervened in this spirit world through ritual ceremonies, in order to produce good fortune, drive away evil, or tell the future. Shamanism has long had a feminine image, and so most *mudang* are women. They dress in elaborate, multi-colored costumes, and sing and dance like dervishes. They convey the words of departed relatives to living family members. And they perform striking feats, such as balancing on knife-blades.

Painting of a shamanic *gut* from the Joseon Dynasty.

A *mudang* in trance, as shown in this photo from the late 19th century.

BECOMING A *MUDANG*

There are two ways to become a *mudang*. Neither is seen as a matter of choice, but rather of destiny. The first is to become possessed by a particular spirit. In the first stages, the potential *mudang* suddenly contracts *shinbyeong*, a "spiritual sickness" which can lead to bizarre and restless behavior. The illness is cured by participating in a *naerim-gut*, a ceremony performed by an older, more experienced *mudang*, which results in the sufferer accepting the incoming spirit. From then on, the former sufferer toils as an apprentice, under the guidance of the older *mudang*. This stage may last several years, until the young *mudang* is ready to lead ceremonies by herself.

The other way is through inheritance. If your mother was a *mudang*, you could learn the techniques she used, and eventually practice them yourself. This tradition was magnified during the Joseon era (1392–1910). Shamanism was treated as backward and false by the Joseon authorities, and thus *mudang* were demoted to the lowest of Korean social classes. One consequence of this was that it became difficult for someone from a *mudang* family to marry a "normal" person, or earn a living in a "normal" way. So they tended to marry each other, and raise their children in the tradition.

The tools of the trade. *Musok* rituals often involve *bukeo* (pollack fish), as well as alcohol as an offering. The bag contains animal entrails.

SHAMANISM: AN EXPENSIVE BUSINESS IN TODAY'S KOREA

Now liberated from the shackles of Joseon oppression, the *mudang* are once again flourishing—even in spite of Korea becoming a modern, industrial society. There are millions of Koreans who will consult with *mudang* on matters such as business, relationships, and the naming of children. Even wealthy *chaebol* (conglomerate) owners have turned to them, as have politicians ahead of crucial elections.

Mudang provide varying levels of service. The basic consultation, or *jeom*, may cost in the tens of dollars, and amount to a simple conversation about the client's destiny, or what they should do about a particular problem. For those with enough money—or serious enough problems—a *gut* may be in order. This is a lengthy ceremony of cathartic song and dance, which directly intervenes with the spirits to produce a beneficial outcome. It is not unheard of for such ceremonies to cost US$10,000 or more.

This means that some *mudang*—particularly the unscrupulous—can become very rich.

A large *gut* in which an animal sacrifice has been offered. Note the three-pronged trident forks. The trident is a common symbol of *musok*.

Mountains and *Mudang*

Mountains are the most spiritually important geographic features of Korean shamanism. Mountains are worshipped individually, and there is even a mountain god, Sanshin. Sanshin is probably the most important among the many countless thousands of gods followed by *mudang*. He is represented as a robe-clad, bearded mystic figure. Portraits of him may also be found in Buddhist temples.

"DON'T BUY A BLUE CAR WHEN YOU'RE 34"

Probably most Koreans would not say "I believe in shamanism." But it has been part of their country's culture for millennia, making for a kind of ingrained, natural belief. There is enough demand to sustain 300,000 *mudang* and other, lesser fortune-tellers. And their advice is taken seriously. When I interviewed one, she told me: "Don't buy a blue car. Especially when you are 34." When I tell friends about this, some of them just laugh—but others give me a very serious look, and implore me never to think about tempting fate.

TRADITIONAL FOLK PAINTINGS (*MINHWA*) AND CRAFTS

A tiger as portrayed in a *minhwa* painting from the Joseon Dynasty. The tiger is the representative animal of old Korea.

The great tragedy of Korean folk art is that nobody knows who produced most of it. Go to a museum showing *minhwa*—traditional Korean folk painting, which usually shows classically Asian-looking scenes of animals and nature—and the label underneath will likely say "Artist Unknown." The *minhwa* style we know today developed in the 1600s, and its practitioners were craftsmen, not famous and well-paid artists.

And like *hanok*, people lost interest in *minhwa* during the era of rapid economic development. Today, *hanok*, *minhwa*, and other forms of traditional Korean art are making a comeback.

Koreans used to look on their history with a sense of shame or disappointment, but now they are discovering that there was also much to be proud of.

Which Traditional Art Forms are Winning New Fans?

BOJAGI This is a kind of square wrapping cloth. This does not sound terribly exciting, but *bojagi* is in fact very striking. It is made with multicolored scraps of fabric arranged in seemingly random fashion, and creates an effect reminiscent of Dutch artist Mondrian's grid paintings.

An unusually complex example of *bojagi*, used by queens during the Joseon Dynasty.

PANSORI

Pansori is a form of song which enjoyed popularity in the late Joseon era. A *sorikkun* (singer) performs accompanied only by a *buk* (a small drum) for as long as eight hours. There are two main lyrical themes. The first is love, such as is found in the "Song of Chunhyang," a classic Korean tale that might be compared to Romeo and Juliet.

The second is satire of the *yangban* aristocratic class. Joseon was a feudal state in which the average person had a rough, downtrodden existence; *Pansori* was the people's way of entertaining themselves whilst venting their frustrations. In 2012, a very modern satirical *Pansori* played in theaters nationwide—*Jui-wang Mollakgi* ("The Fall of the Rat King"), which poked fun at then-president Lee Myung-bak.

Pottery

Korean ceramics have a 10,000 year history, so it is no surprise that this country produces quality pottery. Probably the best known type is *Koryo Cheongja*, which has a highly distinctive green celadon glaze, and sometimes featured elaborate styling and animal motifs. During the Joseon era, tastes were more austere and simple, elegant, white-glazed ceramics came into vogue. During the Japanese invasions of 1592–1598, master potters were abducted and sent to Japan. Their artistic descendants produced the famed Satsuma porcelain.

HANBOK *Hanbok* simply means "Korean dress." For women, it consists of a *jeogeori* (jacket) and a high-waisted skirt, or *chima*. Men also wear *jeogeori* along with *baji* (trousers) and an overcoat, known as a *durumagi*. Traditionally, commoners wore white and royalty wore yellow, though other colors like red, blue, and indigo could also be seen. Traditionally, *hanbok* was big, loose-fitting, and modest; in the case of female *hanbok*, one could say it was deliberately designed to be un-sexy. These days, however, there are haute couture designers like Lee Young-hee, who make short-skirted *hanbok*.

Below A lady in royal *hanbok*. Note the difference in color and complexity between her outfit and the *hanbok* of the fellow on the left.

A game of *nol-ttwigi*, in which participants jump up and down on see-saws, performing back flips and other acrobatic stunts. To do it well, a great deal of skill and confidence is required. I think I would probably break my neck if I tried *nol-ttwigi*!

THE DANO FESTIVAL:
DANCING, SINGING, DRINKING AND WRESTLING

Those who want to see the best elements of "old Korea" in one place should head to a Dano festival. The day of Dano falls on the fifth day of the fifth month of the lunar calendar, and its celebration dates from the days of the Mahan Confederacy, a grouping of pre-unified Korea states that existed from the first century BC until the third century AD. Its purpose was originally to celebrate the end of the crop sowing season, and offer worship to the shaman sky god in the hope of a successful yield.

A *minhwa* painting of a Dano festival. Dano has over a thousand years of history.

The biggest and best-known of such Dano festivals is held at the east coast town of Gangneung (in Gangwon Province). The Gangneung Dano itself has been designated by UNESCO as a "masterpiece of the oral and intangible heritage of humanity," having a history that stretches back over a thousand years.

WHAT HAPPENS AT A DANO?
UNESCO's rather grandiose label belies the real sense of fun found at a Dano. The Dano festival today is a combination of shamanic rites and games. Groups of *mudang* collectively perform mass *gut* rituals replete with manic singing and dancing, to the beat of drums; young women jumping on see-saws turn somersaults ten meters in the air, in a game named *nol-ttwigi*; and wrestlers do battle all day long in Ssireum bouts. But above all, a Dano festival is simply a gathering of people, for the purpose of enjoyment. And to that end, alcohol is never far away. Korea is a drinker-friendly country, and always has been. At a Dano, participants will drink *makgeolli* (rice wine), beer, or *soju*, the most common Korean spirit.

When sufficiently encouraged by these, participants will be up on their feet, dancing to Korean folk songs. Perhaps contrary to expectation, it is mostly old people who enjoy doing this. One will see old men and women swaying from side to side, waving their arms in the air, with jovial grins etched on their faces as they sing along.

Dano are very popular with older people. This old lady plays on a swing, another feature of Dano.

Nol-ttwigi participants are usually women. Legend has it that the game was invented by *yangban* women who wanted to see the world beyond the walls of their home. During the Joseon Dynasty, the role of the woman was often simply that of a housewife.

Eumjugamu: Fun, Fun, Fun!

There is a word that can describe the kind of fun that those old people have at a Dano festival: *eumjugamu*. *Eumjugamu* means "drinking, singing, and dancing," and though it is not something Koreans usually look on with pride, it is an important part of the national culture. Koreans are known for their *han* (a kind of deep melancholy and resentment), but there is also a great amount of pure, for-the-heck-of-it enjoyment to be found here too. The usual means of expressing it is through *eumjugamu*—by singing in *noraebang* (karaoke) rooms, dancing in public parks, or indulging in *natsul* (daytime drinking), for instance.

Koreans today live stressful lives, with long working hours and relentless social pressure to succeed. This means that opportunities to simply cut loose are becoming fewer and fewer. And furthermore, many think *eumjugamu* unsophisticated—not least the tourism authorities, who prefer to focus on either K-pop or traditional arts and crafts when promoting the country. I find this a shame. *Eumjugamu* is one of the most attractive aspects of Korean life.

A Ganggangsullae circle dance, originally a strenuous song-and-dance spectacle performed by unmarried women. These days, Ganggangsullae is more the preserve of the middle-aged and elderly, at Dano and other country festivals. In days gone by, lyrics would be sung that criticized the social order, or Japanese colonial rule.

HANOK: THE TRADITIONAL KOREAN HOME

The *hanok* is a traditional single-story house, constructed of basic materials like wood, stone, and clay. It has slatted wooden doors, which are covered with treated mulberry paper (*hanji*), making them breathable but water-resistant. Classically, the roof of a rich man's *hanok* was tiled, whilst the poor had to make do with thatch. Social superiors such as *yangban* aristocrats also lived at higher altitude than the poor, so they could literally look down upon everyone else from their *hanoks*.

Ideally, one would build one's *hanok* with a mountain to the back, and a river to the front—this is in accordance with an ancient geomantic principle called *baesanimsu*. But the design of the *hanok* itself very much varies by region. In the colder north, they are typically constructed in a square formation, with a courtyard in the middle; this conserves heat, and contrasts with the more open "L" shape found in the south of the peninsula.

Above Nakseonjae area (interior) Changdeokgung, Seoul.

Below Andong-papered door in a *hanok*.

THE DECLINE OF THE *HANOK*

Unfortunately, the dawn of industrial Korea meant the near-death of the *hanok*. Urbanization in Korea meant high-density, high-rise living—something that single-story *hanoks* cannot provide. And for residents, apartments offered convenience. They require little maintenance, with any external work taken care of by a building management company. Heating is simply controlled by a dial, and unlike in an old-style *hanok*, an apartment's toilet is not located outdoors.

Koreans thus began to see the *hanok* as backward. Even in rural towns, where there is much less need to stack people on top of each other, apartment living has become the norm. By the turn of the millennium, there were only about 10,000 *hanoks* left in the whole country. Korean architects regarded these houses—which they themselves grew up in and then left behind—as a curious relic of the past.

THE RESURRECTION OF THE *HANOK*

In the past decade though, a few seeds of change have been sown. The spirit of the development era was of never looking back, and tearing down anything considered "old"—

Arched gate, Seokpajeong Villa, Buam-dong. The Seokpajeong was the villa of Korea's 19th century prince regent, Heungseon Daewongun.

but Koreans now are rediscovering their history and salvaging its best aspects. One result of this has been the preservation of *hanoks*, and even the development of expensive hybrid *hanoks*. Such homes contain modern innovations like electric heating and luxury bathroom suites. There are even hybrid *hanoks* that contain basements and garages, features that never existed traditionally.

Though some criticize modernized *hanoks* as inauthentic, one undoubtedly positive consequence of the trend is the fact that Koreans are now aware of desirable alternatives to the apartment block. Though Korea's high population density means that apartments will always be necessary in urban areas, it would be a positive development if the addiction to aesthetically ugly, gray cookie-cutter tower blocks could be weakened a little.

A Palace Roof at Deoksugung, in Seoul

Traditional Korean roof structures are good for energy conservation: they are curved, providing longer periods of shade when the sun is high in the sky (summer), and allowing light in for longer in the winter. Some Korean architects now argue that such designs are due a revival in the 21st century, on account of their energy efficiency.

Seoul's Bukchon District

The district of Bukchon was long seen as a throwback to old Seoul. As the rest of the city modernized, Bukchon was one of a handful of holdouts where *hanoks* still lined the streets instead of apartment buildings. Living there was dirt cheap, because nobody wanted to own *hanoks*. But due to two factors—the new "cool" factor of hybrid *hanoks*, and generous local government restoration subsidies with few strings attached—Bukchon has now become a boom town. This has resulted in million dollar-plus house prices, and the tearing down of real old-style *hanoks* in favor of concrete structures with *hanok*-esque roofs, in some cases. As a result, battle lines have been drawn between *hanok* "purists," and modernizers bent on redevelopment. Violent clashes have even occurred.

THE KOREAN MARTIAL ARTS:
TAEKWONDO, SSIREUM, AND MORE

Korea's national sport is Taekwondo, a modern martial arts discipline that now takes pride of place at the Olympic Games. The word "Taekwondo" roughly means "the way of the fist and the foot," owing to its strong emphasis on kicks as well as punches. The sport has somewhat political origins: in 1952, president Syngman Rhee ordered the instruction of different martial arts techniques to the army; he later compelled the various schools that emerged to unify, under the Korea Taekwondo Association.

Taekwondo will always be one of the cornerstones of Korea's image abroad. The government estimates there to be around 70 million people practicing the sport worldwide—indeed, Korean fighters no longer have supremacy in it. However, Taekwondo is merely one of a long list of Korean martial arts. Other notable ways to take someone down include:

Top Demonstration of Taekwondo. Middle left Ssireum wrestlers in action. Middle right Drawing of ancient Traditional Taekwondo. Above Son Tae-jin winning Taekwondo gold at the SportAccord Games in Beijing, 2010. Korea of course still produces such champions, but the national sport is now so globalized that winners come from all over the world.

TAEKKYEON

Taekkyeon This is an ancient martial art that predates the nation of Korea itself. Practitioners keep in continual motion, almost dancing around the ring, and use a seemingly endless variety of kicks, throws, knees, locks, and even head butts—although the latter are banned in competition.

SSIREUM

Ssireum This is a type of wrestling, in which the object is to force any above-knee part of your opponent's body to the ground. Ssireum is an old folk sport often found at country festivals, but there are still leagues today. Famous comedian Kang Ho-dong and giant mixed martial arts fighter Choi Hong-man are both former Ssireum champions.

KUMDO

Kumdo When I first arrived in Korea, I taught English at an institute for kids. Some would turn up in white uniforms, and carry sticks. Said sticks would be held aloft and swung back and forth in the same repetitive motion during break times. They were practicing Kumdo, "the way of the sword." This weapon-based martial art is almost identical to Kendo, having been introduced to Korea by colonizing Japanese around the late 1890s.

Kumdo players tend to favor persistent, rapid striking though, whereas Japanese Kendo practitioners are more likely to wait for a golden chance to knock the opponent for six.

Hapkido Like the Japanese martial art of Jujitsu, Hapkido involves not resisting your opponent's moves with your own force, but using his own momentum against him. If an opponent strikes out at you, you assist (and exploit) his forward motion by throwing him. Hapkido is also very eclectic, having techniques in common with other Korean and Japanese fighting styles—grappling in Hapkido has much in common with Judo. And like other Korean martial arts such as Taekwondo, the sport has a wide variety of kicks, such as the well-known low spinning heel kick. Those who progress through the belts will learn how to defend themselves against opponents wielding knives and sticks.

HAPKIDO

PART 3

MODERN
KOREA

Why does nearly everyone live in a gray apartment block? And why do people always want to know how old I am? What's going on here? is a question I often asked in my early days in Korea. Here, I take a look at some of the peculiarities of daily life in the "land of the morning calm" (which is, in fact, anything but calm).

GIRLS IN THE LIMELIGHT: BEAUTY AND PLASTIC SURGERY

These days, even the shape of a woman's jawline seems to be a big deal, sadly. Product marketers have created a word, "V-line," to describe the jawline of an egg-shaped face that one apparently also needs to have in order to be beautiful. Nowadays, there are several products that capitalise on the V-line trend. In my local convenience store, there is a brand of green tea that, according to the label, will give me a V-shaped jawline. Judging by the success of the drink, it seems there are even some people who believe this!

Overall, a woman with a V-shaped jawline (rather than a square one), high nose and cheekbones, big eyes, and a small face, is considered "ideal." In Korea, beauty is basically scientific, rather than being an in-the-eye-of-the-beholder concept, mysterious and subjective. Whether you are beautiful or not depends on whether you can tick off the items on the above checklist. And if you can't, there's always a doctor who can fix it for you.

Korean beauty ideals. The young lady on the left has a "V-line" jaw shape, pale skin, and a more prominent nose than the average Korean woman. In that sense, she represents the modern Korean ideal of feminine attractiveness.

Emulating Western Ideals of Beauty?

Many people say that Korea, being influenced so strongly by the US, has taken on American beauty ideals. Apart from having fair skin, the typical Hollywood actress is considered by Koreans to have a small face. It is also true that Westernized noses—with their high bridges and more prominent protrusion—are considered desirable by Koreans. And the most common cosmetic surgery procedure in Korea is the "double eyelid" job. This results in the eyelid fold that Westerners tend to have.

However, it is also true that Korean tastes in body shape and fashion are rather different to the West. And if you take a quick glance at photos of Korean female celebrities, you will notice that a very distinct, uniform look is emerging. Plastic surgery, make-up techniques, and styling are now so strong in Korea that even Koreans will say that celebrities are starting to look alike. That look is still an Asian look, rather than a Western one—but with certain Western features, such as big eyes and high noses. To me, it is as though Korean celebrities are trying to take what they believe as the best of all worlds.

SMALL FACE, BIG HAPPINESS

"You have a small face! And you're so pale!" This is what Rob, a friend of mine from Britain, was told by a Korean acquaintance. Rob was taken aback by this sudden pronouncement. A look of self-conscious puzzlement came over his features. Was he being mocked? He instinctively raised his hands and began prodding at his cheeks, nose, and forehead.

In Korea though, small faces and pale skin are considered highly attractive. Skin whitening cream is a very popular product. And there is a common form of plastic surgery here based on shaving down the jawbone, to make the face look smaller. One can sometimes see celebrities on TV with tape measures held up to their heads, in demonstration of their fantastically tiny facial dimensions. Those with big faces (and indeed, big heads) are considered rather ugly.

Doesn't he look handsome!

As for my friend Rob, he was much happier after finding out that he had been complimented. But then he wondered, why was this person—another man—saying it to him? In Korea, it is common to praise people for their looks, even in circumstances that may seem inappropriate to those from other countries (though please note, it is often simply said out of politeness). One Korean executive tells me, "I'd just got back from abroad, and went straight to an investment conference here in Seoul. The MC called a speaker up to the podium, and said, 'Doesn't he look handsome?' Then I thought, yeah, I'm definitely back in Korea!"

Above Pop star Jay Park (Park Jae-beom). Left Girls' Generation, Korea's most successful pop group. No large faces (or large heads) here! Below A plastic surgery advert at a Seoul Metro station. Whatever you think of this kind of advertising, it is hard not to marvel at the skill of the surgeon...

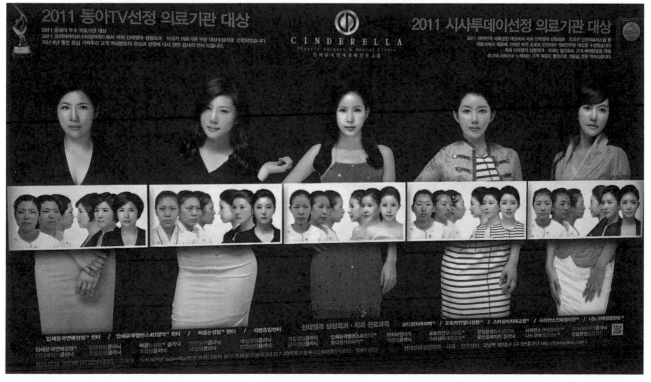

BOYS IN THE LIMELIGHT: THE RISE OF THE PRETTY-BOY

If you've ever watched Korean movies from the 1960s, you'll be familiar with Shin Seong-il. He was the leading man of the era, appearing in such classics of the time as *Barefoot Youth* and *Early Rain*. He was known for playing macho characters who would bounce from bars to street fights to women's bedrooms, usually with a cigarette dangling from his lips. He's still around today, having recently released an autobiography in which he discusses his infidelities and relationship with his long-suffering wife.

1997: A TURNING POINT?

Apparently, the ladies loved a dominant bad boy all the way up to the mid 1990s. But, in the view of James Turnbull, who runs a Korea-focused sociology blog named The Grand Narrative, the economic crisis of 1997–98—known as the "IMF Crisis" to most Koreans—marked a turning point.

Women, he says, bore the brunt of the crisis. Traditionally sexist, Korean society had begun to offer women opportunities in the workplace, but when trouble hit, the assumption was that men needed jobs more than women. Men were seen as the providers, so they took priority. Mr. Turnbull speculates that anger at this may have caused outright rejection of the strong, provider type by Korean women.

Above right Jang Keun-seok, of *You're My Pet* fame. **Far right** Lee Min-ho lauching a new man product at Etude House. **Right** Pop star G-Dragon. **Below** The Face Shop store front in Myeongdong, Seoul, featuring Kim Hyun-joon.

MALE COSMETICS AND PLASTIC SURGERY

Since just before the turn of the millennium then, we have seen a very different kind of "ideal man" in Korea. He doesn't smoke, has probably never been in a fight, and is wrapped around the little finger of his girlfriend. He cares about his appearance, sometimes to the point of wearing make-up. Twenty-one percent of male cosmetics sold worldwide are bought by Korean men. This adds up to US$900 million annually, spent on BB Cream foundation, anti-aging creams, toning serums, etc. Sometimes, when I see Korean boy bands in adverts, I do a double take and ask myself, that one on the left—is he really a guy? 2AM singer Jo Kwon, for instance, is particularly effeminate. These

days, male K-pop stars are almost as likely to have had plastic surgery as their female counterparts, and invariably, the doctor makes them cuter rather than more masculine. Nasal surgery is particularly common.

Left 2AM singer Jo Kwon (left).

Above BB Cream.

Below G-Dragon & T.O.P., members of K-pop group Big Bang.

Left Many men are also having plastic surgery these days. This rather amusing advert is for the surgical removal of "man boobs."

BEING A FOREIGNER IN KOREA: A QUESTION OF PERSONAL SPACE

Korea is becoming quite individualistic these days. But compared to the Western world, the concept of personal space is still noticeably weaker. This can be related to *jeong* culture, and the desire to build up close relations with people. Korea is a group-oriented society, where people like to do things together rather than alone.

Thus, there is a lot more touchy-feely-ness in Korea than in my own country. Do not be surprised if someone you just met for the first time—particularly someone of the older generation—puts their hand on your knee as they talk to you, or grasps your hand. It isn't a sign of creepiness, but rather, a sign that they like you in a friendly way. Similarly, many Koreans are not shy about asking personal questions (see box right).

If you're from a more Anglo-Saxon culture, this shorter distance between people can take a little while to get used to. I have come to appreciate it now, but can still sometimes feel *dabdabhada* (suffocated, or stifled) when someone I don't know very well grabs my hand, or asks me why I am not married!

Awkward Questions

"Why does everyone want to know how old I am?" This is a question several English friends have asked while visiting me in Korea. Where I come from, it can be considered rude to ask someone their age. But in Korea, it is very important to find out how old a person is when you first meet them. This is due to age-based hierarchy, which relates to Confucianism. It will help determine matters like who shows the most respect to who, and who pays for who's meal. But that isn't the only awkward question you might hear from a new acquaintance. On many occasions, people I have just met have wanted to know my religion. I have even been asked, "How much money do you earn?" by folks I barely know. This is particularly true for Westerners in Korea, as there is a widespread suspicion (usually correct, truth be told) that they are overpaid in comparison to locals.

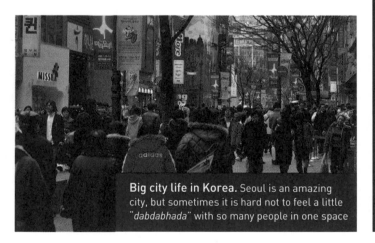

Big city life in Korea. Seoul is an amazing city, but sometimes it is hard not to feel a little "*dabdabhada*" with so many people in one space

Do You Have A Girlfriend? Are You Christian?

A very common awkward question is, "Are you married?" This is not so bad in itself, but if you answer "No," the follow-up will be, "Then, do you have a girlfriend/boyfriend?" If you say "No" again, then you may hear a pitying, "Ah, never mind, you'll meet someone soon"—or even get a detailed description of another singleton they know, someone whom you "really should" meet. You should also be prepared to hear your new friend ask "Why are you single?" And if you try to change the

subject, don't be too shocked if you are met with further questions.

It is a similar story when it comes to religion. I was surprised at first when people would look me in the eye very earnestly, and say, "I am a Christian. What is your religion?" (Note well: in Korea, "Christian" means "Protestant;" Catholicism is treated as a separate thing altogether.) For me, this is the most awkward question of all. Frankly, I'm not religious in any way. Korean Protestants tend to be very evangelical, so there is a strong chance that invitations to church, and special "meetings," will follow. Sometimes, I just tell people I'm a Catholic, to avoid such pressure.

KOREA, THE LAND OF 10,000 COFFEE SHOPS: CAFE CULTURE WITH A VENGEANCE

One thing that visitors to Korea always remark upon is the huge number of coffee shops in this country. Particularly in major cities like Seoul, Busan, and Daejeon, there will be several on each block. The four largest chains have over 2,000 outlets in Seoul between them.

CAFFE BENE

American behemoths like Starbucks are everywhere. But the real lord of the beans in Korea is Kim Seon-kwon, founder of local outfit Caffe Bene. Mr. Kim opened his first store in May 2008, but now has over 800 branches nationwide, making him the market leader. He used his connections in the entertainment industry to draft in stars to cut the ribbon on new stores. Jang Keun-seok of *You're My Pet* fame is one of Caffe Bene's spokes-models.

Caffe Bene is so successful that some call it *bakwi-bene*—*bakwi* being part of the Korean word for "cockroach"—implying that it keeps on spreading, and nothing can kill it. In addition to celebrity marketing, Caffe Bene has also benefited from a wise localization strategy. Stores play mostly Korean pop music, in particular the "ballad" songs that dating couples enjoy. They also sell *patbingsu,* a Korean dessert made from red bean, sugar, and ice—which is actually a lot tastier than my description of it.

WHY SO MANY COFFEE SHOPS?

Though gigantic chains like Caffe Bene have come out of nowhere in the past five to ten years, the coffee shop itself has long been a feature of Korean social life. When I first arrived here, independent stores with private booths were very popular with couples on dates. Movies from the 1960s will often have coffee shop scenes, too. And in a sense, today's Caffe Bene is just a descendant of the old-fashioned Korean coffee house. It is not so much the drink itself, but rather the social function of the cafe that is important. Because of Korea's group orientation, people will usually rather get together somewhere than stay home. Coffee shops are the most convenient place to do that. Also, it is relatively uncommon to visit a friend's home in Korea. In England, I was forever attending house parties, or just dropping in on people. But an invitation to a person's home in Korea is more of a big deal. Nobody says "come round;" instead, they say, "Let's meet at Caffe Bene." And because the vast majority of young, unmarried people live with their parents, time spent with a date will be time spent outside the home—usually in a coffee shop.

The Coffee Shop Perma-lancer

Official unemployment in Korea is very low—around four percent. But these days, a third of the workforce are freelancers, interns, part-timers, or irregular workers. Solid, full-time jobs with large companies are scarce. This is generally bad for Korea—but it is good for owners of coffee shops, since their venues  are becoming office replacements for the growing army of people who work from project to project. If you visit one of the chains offering free Wi-Fi—Starbucks, Caffe Bene, or Holly's, for instance—you will probably see people sat alone, furiously typing away on laptops. One chain though, The Coffee Bean, makes a point of not offering Wi-Fi, or electricity outlets. A manager at one of their stores told me that this is to preserve the social atmosphere of the space.

DEMOCRACY AND DEMONSTRATIONS
PROTEST! PROTEST! PROTEST!

Historic Background

Modern Korean protest culture was born out of student opposition to military dictatorship. Student protestors brought down Syngman Rhee in April 1960. And as President Park Chung-hee (who ruled from 1961 to 1979) became more authoritarian in the 1970s, a university-based movement for democratization started to build again.

But as the actions of the state became more brutal—the post-Park dictator Chun Doo-hwan, for instance, massacred hundreds of protestors at Gwangju in 1980—more and more were ready to take to the streets. By 1987, an anti-government protest in Seoul could draw over a million people. They weren't just "radicals" and communists, as the government said they were: they were also ordinary office workers, and attendees of Catholic churches, for instance. When the movement reached this point, Chun was wise enough to allow proper democratic elections. The first free and fair presidential election of this new era was held in December 1987.

2008, the "Summer of Protest"

On the left, there are growing numbers of anti-globalization protestors, trade unionists fighting job cuts at large *chaebol* conglomerates, and those who oppose just about anything American (the Korea-US Free Trade Agreement, or the construction of military bases, for instance). In 2008's "summer of protest," disparate opponents of conservative president Lee Myung-bak banded together to bring hundreds of thousands of people pouring into downtown Seoul, every night. The spark for this was the resumption of beef imports from the US. Some Koreans believed that American beef was unsafe, spurred on by rather exaggerated media reports about mad cow disease; after the beef protests got going, people angry about all manner of issues—jobs, education, globalization, and so on—joined them. It was an extraordinary summer, but also one that repeatedly saw the city brought to a standstill, and terrified the government due to its sheer scale.

Everybody Wants to Change the World

"Why are Koreans always protesting about something?" I am often asked. Go to Gwanghwamun (Seoul's downtown area) or Yeouido, the location of the national assembly, and you will never fail to see people waving banners and shouting about some perceived injustice.

Sometimes, protestors pitch up tents and stay for months on end.

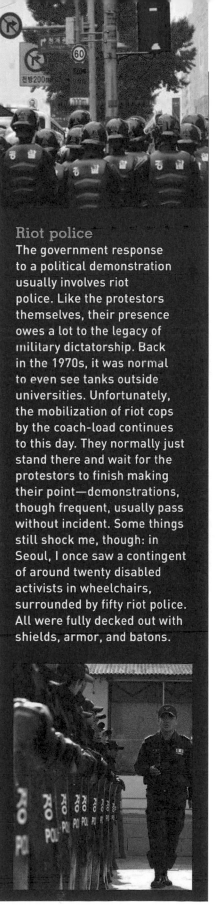

Riot police

The government response to a political demonstration usually involves riot police. Like the protestors themselves, their presence owes a lot to the legacy of military dictatorship. Back in the 1970s, it was normal to even see tanks outside universities. Unfortunately, the mobilization of riot cops by the coach-load continues to this day. They normally just stand there and wait for the protestors to finish making their point—demonstrations, though frequent, usually pass without incident. Some things still shock me, though: in Seoul, I once saw a contingent of around twenty disabled activists in wheelchairs, surrounded by fifty riot police. All were fully decked out with shields, armor, and batons.

DEMO DIVERSITY

Protest in Korea is not just for long-haired students. There is an amazing diversity in terms of age and political inclination among the country's demonstrators. One will always be able to find conservative groups, mostly composed of men in their fifties and sixties, stamping on North Korean flags and burning effigies of Kim Jong-un. *Eobeoi Yeonhap* (Parents United) is one organization that dedicates itself to this, as well as rooting out what it sees as latent communism in South Korean society. To *Eobeoi Yeonhap* though, just about everyone is a communist!

Because Korea is still to fully emerge from the era of rapid construction that began in the 1960s, you can also still see protestors angry about having their district "redeveloped"—i.e. bulldozed, and replaced with expensive apartments they cannot afford. University tuition fees have increased dramatically in recent years, so this brings students out onto the streets as well. And Korean farmers take to protest as readily as their counterparts in other countries.

Though it is easy to criticize Korea's protest culture, the willingness of Koreans to demonstrate is directly linked to the democratization of the country. It is no coincidence that Korea has the liveliest and most competitive democracy in Asia.

Speakers' Corner Seoul Mayor Park Won-soon established this "speakers' corner" in downtown Seoul in 2011. Mayor Park is himself a former activist, having been sent to jail in the 1970s for opposing President Park Chung-hee's regime.

THE SELLING OF *HAHM* AND THE CHANGING KOREAN LIFESTYLE

Not so long ago, most Koreans lived in villages. Cries of "*hahm saseyo!*" would bring local people out into the streets (see box right), giving the *hahmjinabi* a lively audience as he attempted to sell the box to the bride's family. In today's urbanized Korea, though, most people have no relationship at all with their neighbors. And entering an apartment block and selling *hahm* would be considered a noisy intrusion by many residents. For that reason, it is more of a country tradition than a city one today.

Above and left A traditional wedding. Unfortunately, this is also a ceremony in decline. Weddings nowadays are a kind of Korean-Western hybrid. A friend of mine once remarked, "If you see a traditional Korean wedding these days, one of the couple will be a foreigner." **Below** A wedding procession from the late 19th century.

He Puts What on His Face?

As with any country, Korea has a whole host of matrimonial traditions. The one I find most interesting is the selling of *hahm* prior to the wedding.

The selling of *hahm* has very formal origins. The groom's family would prepare a mother-of-pearl inlaid *hahm* (box) filled with cloth, and send it to the bride's family home. The *hahm* was handled with care, and if the family were wealthy enough, it would even be conveyed by servants.

Over the years though, *hahm*-selling turned into a raucous evening activity. It is now conducted by friends of the groom, whose job it is to go around making as much noise as possible, shouting "*hahm saseyo!*" ("please buy *hahm*") in the street outside the bride's home. They also sing songs to ward off bad spirits. There is a group leader, the *hahmjinabi*, who carries the *hahm* on his back, and believe it or not, wears a squid on his face, as a mask.

When the group reach the bride's home, the *hahmjinabi*'s job is to negotiate a generous payment for the *hahm*. He will loudly scorn their initial offers, creating an amusing spectacle on the doorstep. When a deal is finally made, he enters the house and places the *hahm* on a base of red-bean ricecake (by rule, the *hahm* must never touch the ground during the whole sequence of events). He will then bow to the bride's family.

The box is then opened, and gifts such as jewelry and silk are taken out. There will also be a letter, written from the groom's family to that of the bride. This completes the "sale," and the bride can then emerge from her room. At this point, the groom's friends and the bride's family enjoy a lavish feast, with plenty of alcohol laid on for good measure.

SEOUL (AND BUSAN AND DAEJEON AND DAEGU AND GWANGJU): A CITY OF TOWER BLOCKS

With 50 million people squashed into a small land area—around 70 percent of which is mountainous—space is at a premium in Korea. To make matters worse, half of those 50 million are concentrated in or around the Seoul metropolitan area. It is natural, then, that people should live stacked on top of each other, in apartment buildings. All across the land, gigantic towers dominate the skyline. Even in smaller towns and cities, the standard place of residence is an apartment rather than a house. Traditionally, Koreans lived in *hanoks*. The first apartments did not come until the 1930s, when the colonizing Japanese built low-rise blocks for their (Japanese) workers. Koreans were building them in Seoul by the 1940s, but it was not until the days of Park Chung-hee and industrialization that the real change began.

President Park wanted people to get out of the countryside, and move to big cities like Seoul. There, they would work all day long in factories, toiling away to build the nation into an industrial powerhouse. Overpopulation meant

apartments became more suitable than houses. Also, apartments are a lot easier to maintain, so they were a godsend for the overworked laborer.

The Mapo Apartments at Dohwa-dong in the Mapo district of Seoul was the first major apartment complex development, and was completed in 1964. Each building in the complex hand only six floors, due to the lack of elevators. But by the 1980s, tall was the norm, and today, thirty-story apartment buildings are unexceptional. Because Korea was in a rush to industrialize, little consideration was given to aesthetics and build quality. The average apartment complex is full of gray, boxy towers that have no individual character. There are not many parks and open spaces. But in certain areas, these gray boxes are now worth fantastic sums of money.

A TOWN OF REAL ESTATE LOTTERY WINNERS

The citizens of Apgujeong (in the Gangnam district), for instance, were great beneficiaries of property price inflation. Fifty years ago, the area was mostly cheap farmland—priced at around a measly 400 won (roughly 40 cents) per *pyeong* (a unit equivalent to 35 square feet/3.3 square meters). But the government decided to develop Gangnam by building good schools. Parents flocked to live there in the new apartments that were being constructed by the likes of Hyundai. Over time, Apgujeong became considered a fancy area, and today, it is full of expensive restaurants, luxury brand fashion shops, and plastic surgery clinics. The Apgujeong Hyundai apartments still stand, and cost at least a billion won (one million US dollars) each to buy now. In the 1970s, Seoul apartments could be snapped up for less than a hundredth of that. This trend has been wonderful for the older generation. But for younger Koreans trying to purchase homes today, it makes life very difficult.

Above Area near Gangnam Station, Seoul **Below** Apgujeong, also in Gangnam. Apgujeong is famed for its massive property boom, which made apartment owners rich in the 1980s and 1990s.

Seoul 100 years ago

Modern Seoul

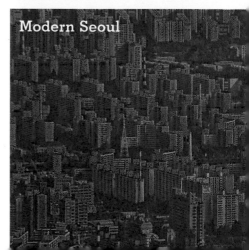

PART 4

KOREA'S
INTERNET
MANIA

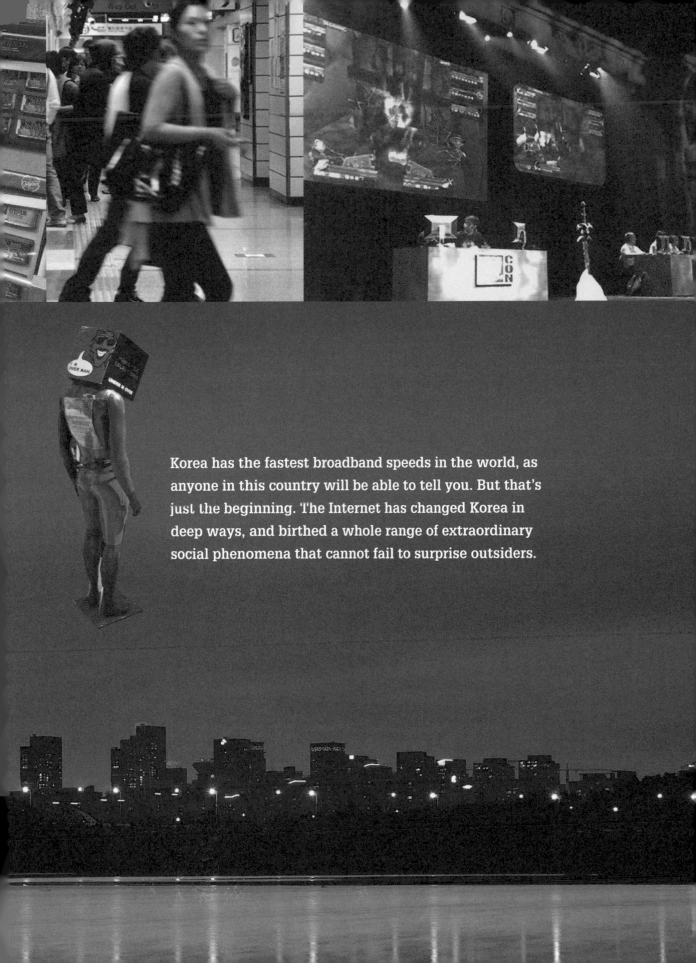

Korea has the fastest broadband speeds in the world, as anyone in this country will be able to tell you. But that's just the beginning. The Internet has changed Korea in deep ways, and birthed a whole range of extraordinary social phenomena that cannot fail to surprise outsiders.

THE POWER OF THE INTERNET

Since the dawn of the Internet age, there has been endless discussion in Korea about the power of the "netizen." As the name would suggest, a netizen is simply an Internet user. But the word also tends to conjure up someone who inhabits online forums, offering opinions and spreading negative press and misinformation about celebrities, politicians, and any other high-profile person unlucky enough to earn his ire.

Korea is a society in which outspoken, public criticism is generally taboo. If you attack someone publicly, you can expect them to take it very personally. Perhaps because of this, laws on libel and slander are extremely strict. The Internet, though, allows for a strong degree of anonymity, breaking through the taboo. The online forum gives the angry netizen a way to vent without consequence. Thus it has become common for celebrities to earn "anti-fans"—people who have nothing better to do than entertain themselves by grouping together and attacking famous people.

POLITICAL CLOUT

One of the most popular websites in Korea is called Ilbe. Its users—so-called "Ilbe Bugs"—are known as far-right fanatics who love nothing more than expressing sexist opinions about women, swearing, and spreading rumors. But the fact that there are around a million Ilbe Bugs means that collectively, they have a certain level of influence in society. They are also known for their insult war with members of the Ddanzi Ilbo website, who have politically opposing views.

Online political clout works in both directions, though. In 2002, liberal candidate Roh Moo-hyun was trailing Lee Hoi-chang (of the Grand National Party, now Saenuri), and few expected him to win. However, a group of netizen fans calling themselves *Nosamo* (people who love Roh Moo-hyun) mounted an all-out online campaign to encourage young people to vote for their hero. Mr. Roh ended up as President Roh, claiming victory by a margin of two percent.

MINERVA UNMASKED

Some netizens have even gained hero status for themselves. A man nick-named "Minerva" became known as a kind of economic prophet in 2008, after posting a series of gloomy predictions about the Korean currency and stock markets. He was correct often enough to gain a massive following, and terrified the government with further prognostications about the collapse of the Korean won. Financial policymakers in Korea are extremely sensitive to criticism, and so an investigation was set up to unmask Minerva's identity. Minerva was well-versed in economic theory and the state of the Korean economy, so there were many who believed him to be a senior bank executive or government insider. However, he turned out to be one Park Dae-sang, a thirty-year-old unemployed man who still lived with his parents. Regardless, the government prosecuted him on charges of "spreading false information." In a victory for civil liberties, the government lost in court. Mr. Park later ending up getting a job as a newspaper columnist.

Your online enemies know who you are, but you don't know who they are. Anonymity is the best friend of the angry netizen.

ANT INVESTORS

There are millions of amateur investors in Korea, who trade online. Professionals disdain them with the nickname *gaemi-deul* (ants). The typical *gaemi* investor is a housewife, or a company worker who slacks off from his duties and plays the stock market instead. Over time, almost all of them lose money, according to research by Samsung Securities, as quoted in *The Hankyoreh* newspaper.

There are many legendary stories about *gaemi* investors and the people who take advantage of them. A cheeky company boss even issued a press release saying that top actress Lee Young-ae had invested in his firm's stock; the first she heard about that was when she picked up a newspaper and read about it on a flight out of Incheon Airport. That did not stop the stock from rocketing, though.

One unscrupulous businessman I met in the mid-2000s actually made it his business to take over small companies and hype them up—announcing their entrance into "hot" markets like education or e-commerce—to draw *gaemi* investors in. Once the price had gone up enough, he would simply sell everything.

Such behavior exists wherever there are stock markets. But in Korea, the sheer popularity of rumor-laced online forums makes for particularly rich pickings for scammers.

TO THE MOON AND BACK

In 2011, politician Moon Jae-in began to be considered a serious candidate for the 2012 presidential election. Some trickster circulated a picture of Mr. Moon online, showing him sat with a man identified as the CEO of a small clothing firm named Daehyun. The photo was accompanied by text stating that if Mr. Moon became president, it would obviously be positive for Daehyun stock—since he was such good friends with the CEO.

Political "theme stocks" such as Daehyun are known to rocket when the connected politician's fame rises. It is certainly unclear whether such a link to the president would enable them to sell more clothes, but in any case, the man in the picture was not even Daehyun's CEO! However, that did not stop the stock from increasing over 200 percent in a matter of weeks.

Daehyun eventually fell back to its original price, causing big losses to those *gaemi* investors who bought in after the rumor started. As for the man who started the rumor, why do you think he did it? He had been quietly buying up Daehyun stock for weeks, and after the rumor came out, he was able to sell for a profit of around a billion won (almost a million US dollars). The authorities did catch up with him later, though.

A Lucky Gentleman Indeed

Remember "Gangnam Style"? There are certainly many small investors who do. Psy's father is the owner of a stock exchange-listed company named DI, and when the horse dance became a global phenomenon in August and September 2012, the price of DI stock shot up by almost 500 percent. It later came back down to earth, causing losses to those who bought in too late. There was no genuine reason for DI's big move. DI makes semiconductors, and experienced no benefit from "Gangnam Style." But small investors in Korea, who spend all day online checking out the latest rumors and fast-action stocks, love to buy such *jakjeon-ju* ("mission" stocks) in search of a quick profit. In the run-up to Psy's follow-up single "Gentleman," DI stock went through the roof once again!

THINK YOU CAN DO BETTER?

On the positive side, there are a lot of excellent companies in Korea, and many are undervalued on the stock market. An investor can actually do very well by doing a little research and of course, avoiding the up-and-down *gaemi* stocks.

Online brokers in Korea are also very fast, efficient, and cheap. I sometimes invest in Korean stocks, and buy them through an online brokerage that charges me about 1,000 won (US$1) per trade. So if you think you can do better than the *gaemi-deul*, why not come and try it for yourself?

THE VIDEO GAMER'S SECOND HOME

When I first lived in Seoul back in 2004, I found it hard to get my bearings in this gigantic city of 10, 14, or 25 million people (depending on how you measure it). So, I was constantly asking people for directions. If I asked a foreign friend, they would sometimes joke, "Turn left at the PC-bang, then take that road until you see another PC-bang, then turn right, and you'll find it on the first floor of the building with that big PC-bang." Or something like that. In 2008, there were 22,000 such places in Korea.

THE PC-BANG: WHAT IS IT?

On one level, the PC-bang is simply an Internet cafe. You go in, pick up a code number at the front desk, and sit down at one of many identical computers lined up in rows. After entering the code, you are free to use the Internet for as long as you like. And when you are done, the code system lets the manager know how much time you used, so he knows how much to charge you. One hour should cost somewhere between 1,000 and 2,000 won.

But what made PC-bangs spring up on every street? The PC-bang story is inseparable from the rise of online gaming. For over a decade, Korean teenagers have been obsessive players of MMORPG games, including many Korean-made titles like Maple Story, Starcraft, and Lineage. And perhaps because Korea is a "collective" society, people sometimes don't want to play alone. Going with friends to a PC-bang and competing against each other in an MMORPG—whilst being able to yell "Ha! You lose!" directly into their ear—is a fun and cheap way to spend an afternoon.

The sign for *bang* in PC-bang. *Bang* simply means "room."

PC-BANG ADDICTS

There are many infamous instances of people taking their PC-bang addiction too far. While it is considered problematic that there are kids playing hooky from school and spending the day in a PC-bang, the stories that generate the most headlines are more extreme. There was a tragic case in 2010 involving a couple whose baby daughter starved, because they spent so much time in the PC-bang that they neglected to feed her. Ironically, the game they were playing involved raising a "virtual child." And there have been other cases of gamers suddenly dying after 48-hour gaming sessions without sleep or food.

For most people though, the PC-bang represents good, honest fun. It is a place to forget about the stress of school and work life by blasting away at monsters. There are also those who use the

If you see the letters "PC" on a building in Korea, you can be 99 percent certain that you've arrived at a PC-bang.

PC-bang for Internet dating: during the mid-2000s, meeting websites like Sayclub grew in popularity, and one could often see PC-bang users video-chatting to strangers or even arranging *beongae*—sudden face-to-face meetings.

END OF THE ROAD?

Perhaps sadly, the PC-bang is in decline these days. Increased government regulation due to gaming addiction, the growth of public Wi-Fi in cafes, and the rise of smartphone-based gaming, pushed their numbers down to around 15,000 by 2010. I suspect that there are even fewer now. If you do visit Korea, make sure you spend an hour in a PC-bang—they are a great Korean institution, and one that might not be around forever.

THE DECLINE AND REBIRTH OF PROFESSIONAL COMPUTER GAMERS

Throughout the early and mid 2000s, Starcraft (made by Blizzard Games) was by far the top game in Korea. Starcraft contests were broadcast on TV, and its top players made fortunes; no other game could come close in terms of popularity and influence. At the top of the Starcraft pyramid stood Ma Jae-yoon, a man so gifted that the rules of Starcraft had to be changed to make it harder for him to win—though even then, he still did. Fans called him "Maestro," and one TV commentator even called him "God."

E-sports contest

All this makes what happened in 2010 even more shocking. Ma Jae-yoon and ten other players were caught fixing Starcraft matches. Why? Although sports gambling is illegal in Korea (other than in strictly regulated government-controlled betting shops that most gamblers don't use)—there are many illegal websites offering odds on all sporting events, including Starcraft. They are run by Korean exiles from places like the Philippines. There is therefore a great incentive to form match-fixing syndicates, as has also happened recently in the Korean football and baseball leagues.

The image of Starcraft had been sullied. Fans didn't know if they could believe what they were watching any more. The popularity of the game declined, and since Starcraft was the flagship e-sports game, it seemed that professional e-sports itself might die.

E-SPORTS TODAY

Luckily, the vacuum was filled by a new game, League of Legends. Its maker, Riot Games, deliberately set out to make a Starcraft-replacing, dominant game, according to "The Korean" of Ask a Korean, probably the best English language blog on Korean culture. Eleven thousand people bought tickets to watch a single League of Legends tournament in 2012, so it is safe to say that Riot Games are on course to achieving their aim. Professional e-Sports may never fully relive its Starcraft-driven golden age. But still, there remain three cable TV channels offering coverage of professional gaming leagues. Competition for front row seats at contests like the annual World Cyber Games—which started in Korea and is still dominated by Korean players—is intense. Players must sit in soundproofed glass cages, so that the screams of the crowd do not distract them.

From left to right
Global Starcraft 2 League; Ma Jae-yoon in action; an Azubu team member competes at a League of Legends competition.

Slay a Dragon, Become a Millionaire

South Korea has become famous, notorious even, for the enthusiasm of its people for computer games. It is perfectly normal here for twenty- and thirty-something men and women to spend hours on MMORPG games. These days, smartphone gaming is also taking off: travel on any metro train or bus, and you will find that at least half of the passengers will be fiddling furiously with an iPhone or Galaxy S, lining up diamonds in rows, or shooting at aliens.

Some take gaming to great extremes. The government has poured tens of millions of dollars into anti-gaming addiction programs. Tales are legion of youngsters who bunk off from school to spend all day playing Counterstrike, Maple Story, or Sudden Attack in their local PC-bang, and throw violent tantrums when their parents try to stop them. But sometimes, these anti-social super-geeks end up as heroes.

The very best gamers in Korea make six-figure incomes. Their faces are emblazoned on posters in children's bedrooms up and down the land. Without any trace of irony, fans call them "e-Sports athletes." Top gamers form teams and attract sponsorship; *chaebols* of course have the deepest pockets so there are Samsung, SK Telecom, and STX teams who participate in Korean e-Sports Association (KeSPA) leagues.

Lee "MarineKing" Jung Hoon and his teammates from team Prime during a match against team oGs.

MarineKing

In 2012, one famous Starcraft player, MarineKing (Lee Jung-hoon), became the subject of an in-depth CNN report. For years, Mr. Lee battled with his parents over his desire to be a professional gamer. They wanted him to grow up to become a judge. He eventually won, and at the age of just nineteen, he is now one of around 700 people in Korea to make a living from pro gaming. He earns around US$100,000 per year, and is besieged by autograph hunters at competitions.

That figure puts MarineKing in the top five percent of pro gaming earners. As with other sports, only the very best make real money. There are some who make more: MarineKing's big rival MVP (21-year old Jung Jong-hyun) makes around a quarter of a million. And even back in the early 2000s, legendary player Lim Yo-hwan was making around US$300,000 per year in sponsorship and winnings.

GOOGLE-BLOCKERS: KOREA'S WORLD CLASS INTERNET COMPANIES

When it comes to top Internet businesses, Silicon Valley still rules the roost. But as may be expected for a country that has the world's fastest broadband and legions of online game maniacs, Korea has a few heavyweights of its own.

NHN You may not have heard of NHN. But it has a stock market valuation of around US$12 billion, as a result of its power in online search and games. Its most famous service is the search engine and portal naver.com, which dominates the market in Korea. In most countries, Google has displaced local competitors, but not here. Why is this? One NHN investor told me, "People doubted Naver, but I searched it for *bi* (the Korean word for "rain") one day, and it came back with lots of information about the pop star (Rain). I did the same on Google, and it just told me about the weather. So then I realized Naver understands Korea." He also notes that the "busy" design suits Korean tastes, in comparison to Google's minimalist layout.

NCSoft and Nexon NHN has also been selling online games since 1999, through its Hangame portal. But who develops the games? The leaders in this field are NCSoft and Nexon. NCSoft was founded by Kim Taek-jin in 1997, and is responsible for hit games like Blade and Soul, Lineage, and Guild Wars. Mr. Kim sold a big stake in his firm to rival Nexon in 2012.

The game-maker Kim Taek-jin.

Nexon has introduced its own virtual currency, NX-Cash, which game players use to trade "virtual items" such as swords, shields, and special powers. This has made Nexon one of the pioneers of "free-to-play" or "freemium" gaming, in which players can experience the basic functions of the game, but upgrade their experience by making (hopefully frequent) small payments. This has proven a highly successful business model, with Western gaming giants now adopting it themselves (Nexon made over US$500 million in 2012, on the back of huge profit margins). Nexon's most famous games include Kart Rider, Maple Story, Sudden Attack, and Counter-Strike.

Daum Another notable firm is Daum ("Next" in Korean), which used to be the leader in search engines, but ended up losing its position to Naver. Daum still operates Hanmail though, the country's most popular email service. Its virtual "cafes" serve as meeting rooms for people with shared interests from politics to homebrewing—this has given Daum a certain amount of social power in Korea.

Daum bosses caused a huge surprise in 2004 by moving their headquarters from Seoul to Jeju Island. Some workers hated this at first, but ended up getting used to the beautiful scenery and cheaper living. In the years to come, I think Daum will be seen as an innovator for pioneering the move away from the capital—something that this seriously Seoul-centric country would benefit from.

VCNC and the Second Wave

NHN, Daum, and NCSoft are all part of the "first wave" of Korean Internet firms. In the 2010s, a "second wave" began to emerge. KakaoTalk (see below) is probably the most successful of these. The one I find most interesting, though, is Value Creators & Company (VCNC), who have developed a "social network for couples," that allows the besotted to share romantic messages and photos, and reminds them of anniversaries and other special dates. They have around four million registered users, and recently attracted US$3 million of venture capital investment from Japanese goliath Softbank.

Dog Poo Girl and Friends

Around half the Korean population uses smartphones. The era of the phone-that-is-also-a-computer has many implications for all of us. For example: you can no longer expect to do anything silly or embarrassing in public without someone secretly filming it. And because Koreans love the Internet and social media, a video taken of you doing something sufficiently amusing will go viral before you can say "Gangnam Style."

The so-called "smoking woman" of the Seoul Metro.

Daum's HQ, which is considered one of Korea's most impressive buildings.

BE CAREFUL WHAT YOU DO ON THE METRO!

As may be expected then, Korea has a number of reluctant cyber-celebrities who came to public attention by doing stupid things. The Seoul Metro seems to be a breeding ground for this. The most (in)famous case was that of the delightfully-named "dog poo girl," who took her pet on the subway, and allowed it to defecate in the carriage. Though challenged by other subway users, she refused to clean up its mess. Unbeknownst to her, the whole incident was being filmed by another passenger.

A few hours later, "dog poo girl" was one of the most-searched topics on the naver.com portal. Netizens conducted a vigilante-type search to uncover her identity. After being "outed," the young woman quit her university and went into hiding, unable to cope with the torrent of abuse unleashed at her, both online and by people who recognized her in public.

Other famous Seoul Metro cases include that of a woman who drank *soju*

Louis Vuitton bags, regulation issue for the so-called *doenjang-nyeo*.

and smoked cigarettes in front of other passengers; a drunken old man who asked a short-skirt clad young woman to participate in group sex with him; and a woman who took her clothes off in the carriage. All of these people were the subject of netizen witch-hunts.

DOENJANG-NYEO AND THE SEXISTS

One important point about viral infamy in Korea is that the subject is, more often than not, a woman. "Sexual harassment Granddad," as the website Koreabang.com calls the old man in the above example, is an exception. The reason for this apparent sexism is that a significant proportion of angry netizens (such as "Ilbe Bugs") are young men who cannot find girlfriends.

Such netizens are especially fond of criticizing the young women they fail to attract as *doenjang-nyeo* ("bean-paste girl"). This word comes from the notion that there are many materialistic women who are so devoted to buying luxury handbags and other showy accessories that they can afford to eat only the

cheapest foods, such as *doenjang-jjigae* (bean-paste stew). This is no longer just an Internet word, though: *doenjang-nyeo* has crossed into the mainstream, and can now be used to describe any young lady who thinks she is a princess.

NETIZEN SLANG: *EOLJJANG* OR *ANYEODWAE*?

Many examples of netizen slang have crossed over into mainstream society. The *eoljjang* of the title is one such word. *Eol* is the first syllable of *eolgul*, the Korean word for "face," and *jjang* simply means "great," or "awesome." So, an *eoljjang* is simply someone who is extremely beautiful or handsome. There is also *momjjang*—*mom* means "body."

When these two words took off, there developed a fad for posting up photos of models, actors and actresses, and members of the public, on online forums; this was done to determine by netizen consensus who was the greatest *eoljjang* or *momjjang*. Among Korean actresses, Jun Ji-hyun would be considered an ideal example of the former, and Kim Hye-soo the latter.

Everyone in Korea knows these two words. But fewer know *anyeodwae*, which has a rather cruel, and opposite, meaning. This one is a contraction of the Korean words for "spectacles," "acne," and "pig." Perhaps thankfully, it did not become a mainstream word. Here are some other examples of Internet slang.

Internet Slang

Though it takes me a while, I can read a Korean newspaper. Unfortunately, I have much more serious difficulty deciphering the content of online forums, Twitter messages, and Daum "cafe" posts. This is due to the huge amount of slang and Internet-specific vocabulary that Korean Internet users employ.

2MB This refers to former president Lee Myung-bak. The number "2" in Korean has the same pronunciation as "Lee," and the "MB" comes from "Myung" and "bak." Since a computer with 2MB of memory would be considered pitifully slow, the expression was used as an insult against the president's intellectual capacity.

The Korean character ㅋ Or sometimes, its Roman alphabet soundalike "k," simply means "haha." You can use as many ㅋ or "k" as you like, depending on how funny something is. So if you receive an email from a Korean containing the letters "kkk," please be assured that they are not referring to the Ku Klux Klan (I have heard of such a conclusion being made).

Gaedokgyo The Korean word for "Christianity" is *gidokgyo*. But the word for "dog" is *gae*, which isn't a million miles away from sounding like *gi*. So, netizens who dislike Christianity are able to label church-goers as dog religionists.

Jwa-jom and **Jong-buk** These are words right-wing "Ilbe bugs" use to describe those on the left. *Jwa* means left, and *jom* refers to "zombie," suggesting a person blind to anything other than hardcore socialism. *Jong-buk* means someone "in thrall to the North" (i.e. North Korea).

KIN When I first lived in Seoul back in 2004, I taught English. My younger students were constantly writing "KIN" on the blackboard, on their folders, on each others' folders, on textbooks, and on tables. If you turn "KIN" ninety degrees to the right, it looks like the first syllable of the Korean for "enjoy your chatting"—which was actually a euphemistic Internet chatroom expression for "get lost." The makers of a soft drink also named "KIN" (going since 1976) cannot have been too happy about all this, but like most manias, KIN was a short-lived one.

OTL This is a visual piece of slang, used to express great disappointment or shock. If you can't guess why, imagine a man bent over, banging his head against the floor. Now look at the letters again.

Teu-chin This is a contraction of the words that mean "Twitter Friend" in Korean. Twitter is now extremely popular among young people, especially those who are interested in politics. In Korea, this social networking service is mainly a conduit for political information and misinformation. Progressives dominate but increasingly, conservatives are also becoming active on Twitter.

Yeolpok A contraction of the words *yeoldeunggam pokbal*, which means "explosion of inferiority complex." If one forum user criticizes a rich or famous person, you can reply *Yeolpok!*, as if to say, you're just jealous!

Deceased North Korean dictator Kim Jong-il. If you like this guy, you're definitely a *jong-buk*.

Above what KakaoTalk looks like. Right President Obama, apparently a Kakao fan.

KAKAOTALK—JUST GETTING STARTED

But Kakao Inc., the company behind KakaoTalk, is only just getting started. Because its messaging service is free, Kakao can't make money directly from it—but it can "monetize" its gigantic user base through advertising, and the offering of additional services. Developers are able to sell mobile games through Kakao, taking advantage of a guaranteed target audience of millions—for which Kakao earns a commission. And in 2012 the firm also rolled out KakaoStory, a simple social network that gained ten million users in a matter of weeks.

Also in 2012, Kakao's move to introduce free voice calls through its app caused panic among Korea's cellular carriers. KakaoTalk has already eaten their SNS revenues, and if their call minutes revenue disappears too, their whole business model will be in doubt. For now, the audio quality of such voice calls is not quite up to scratch—but one day, I'm sure it will be. The Korean Communications Commission is thus taking great interest in Kakao's ambitious project.

Kakao Inc.'s founder, Kim Beom-soo, also started Hangame—a major game portal that was eventually merged into NHN. But today, he must compete with NHN: that firm, Korea's largest in the IT sector, has its own free messaging and voice-call app, Line. Line is dwarfed by KakaoTalk in Korea, but does have millions of users in Japan, Thailand, and China.

Services like KakaoTalk and Line have grown in tandem with the smartphone.

We Used to Talk, Now We Just KakaoTalk

The SMS, or text message, is dead and buried in Korea. The killer was KakaoTalk, a free messaging app for smartphones. For those with data plans, Kakao offers a way to send unlimited messages to friends anywhere in the world, at no cost. A majority of the Korean population uses Kakao, and at the time of writing, the service had around another 50 million users worldwide, operating in English, Chinese, Spanish, Turkish, Italian, and other languages.

Well over three billion messages are sent back and forth between users each day. If you have Korean friends, you will definitely want to download KakaoTalk. Even US President Barack Obama talks about it—during his speech at the Hankuk University of Foreign Studies in 2012, he referenced the app, making the assembled crowd of students scream with delight.

Mr. Kim the Venture Capitalist

Kim Beom-soo meanwhile wears another hat. Thanks to his Hangame and Kakao millions, he has become one of Korea's leading venture capitalists. Funding from his K-Cube Ventures fund is highly sought after by young tech entrepreneurs. K-Cube now has a "family" of twelve small companies. One example is the funkily-named social network service Vingle, itself founded by Moon Ji-hoon of Viki—a popular streaming TV site that offers translated versions of Korean dramas.

An Interview with Simon and Martina of "Eat Your Kimchi"

Simon and Martina Stawski are a husband-and-wife video-blogging team who have probably done more to promote popular Korean culture than the Korean government. Their website, Eatyourkimchi.com, is a traffic phenomenon—especially when they interview K-pop stars. The Stawskis have even been mobbed getting off the plane in Mexico, as though they were the Beatles...

Why did you start making Eat Your Kimchi (EYK)? Were you trying to do something "big," or did that occur by chance?
We just started it out to keep our families informed about what we were doing in Korea. We heard in the news that North Korea threatened South Korea with an "Ocean of Fire" right before we got on the plane, so everyone was a bit worried. We started making videos to show them that everything's ok, and that they wouldn't have to worry. We had no plans on it getting any bigger than that!

What is the most popular type of content on your site?
Our K-pop segments are the most popular, though our adventure segments are close behind.

Can you please tell me some instances of netizen mania that you have encountered because of EYK? Have you been drowned in gifts, sent hate-mail, been mobbed in the street, stalked, or anything like that?
We get a lot of overwhelming support from our audience. It shocks us, because we just feel like we're two dorks who make videos in our apartment, so when people talk to us outside, in "the real world" so to speak, we're taken aback. When we were in California for the Google MBC K-pop concert, that's when it hit us the most. After the event, we tried to leave the amphitheater to get to the parking lot, but we were swarmed by people asking us for pictures and autographs. They had shirts made with our pictures on them. They held up placards with our names on them. We were swarmed to the point that we really couldn't actually move. A two-minute walk to the parking lot took 45 minutes. We never knew that people would be so interested in seeing us!

On the more negative side, we've had some very nasty trolls on the Internet say terrible things about us. When it first started happening, we almost wanted to quit and just leave. Fortunately, we didn't, but it's still hard for us to deal with when we see it online.

Why do you call your fans "Nasties"? :-)
Ha! We thought for a long time about a fangroup name. For starters, we didn't even want to have a fangroup name. Fangroups are for celebrities with talent. We're neither celebrities nor talented. So, if we did have a fangroup name, it's not something we could take too seriously, like "Angels" or "Darling Sunshines" or something like that.

The idea for "Nasties" came about because "OOOH YOU SO NASTY!" is a kickphrase we use whenever we talk about something awkwardly sexual in K-pop Music Videos, and try to imitate it awkwardly ourselves. So, we figured, why not call the fangroup the nasties? The kickphrase could be the calling card. It acknowledges the one-ness with the fangroup, but it's also a bit self-deprecating and ironic, you know?

How much is K-pop part of your success? And generally, what kind of future do you see for K-pop (i.e. will it be the kind of mega global success story that many people here want it to be)?
That's difficult for us to say. I know we're most popular for our K-pop videos, which I think is in part because there aren't many people who do what we're doing, but our other videos are really successful as well, and oftentimes get more views than our K-pop videos. As for the future of K-pop, it's so difficult for us to predict. We are thinking that it's going to start looking into following a more organic route, as in the examples of Psy and [pop-rock band] Busker Busker, who make great music on their own without their companies making the songs for them.

What other blogs and Korea-related sites can you recommend for people wanting to know more about Korea?
We really like what Hyunwoo Sun is doing over at [Korean language-learning website] TalkToMeInKorean.com. We also like to keep up to date with Korean news via the Marmot's Hole [another popular blog, found at www.rjkoehler.com] and Reddit's Korea sub-Reddit.

Very briefly, please imagine a young person asks you, "Why should I visit Korea?" What would you tell them?
What you've grown up with isn't how things are everywhere. Travel to Korea, see a different side of the world, how things are done differently. You'll start to question what you're used to and think is universally accepted, but you'll also learn to appreciate different things you've taken for granted.

The government here is always trying to promote and brand Korea, it seems. What do you think of their efforts? If they put you in charge of it, what would you do differently?
We're trying to take a different approach than what we've seen from the Korean government. From our perspective, it just seems like they're interested in promoting Korea's traditional stuff. Tourists should come to Korea, go to the temples and mountains, wear a *hanbok* and make *kimchi*. And while, sure, that may be for some people, we feel like Korea's more modern side is a bit neglected. We like talking about Korea's coffee shops, their indie and art scene, their students. Korea's got a very young and vibrant culture, but you wouldn't know that from looking at how Korea's regularly promoted.

What plans do you have for the future? Will you stay in Korea, or go on to Drink your Sake, Slurp your Pho, etc?
We had plans to move to Japan and start "Eat Your Sushi," but we've dropped that now. We're in Korea for the long run. We just registered as a business in Korea and bought a studio in Hongdae. We're going to have more video segments, bring in a staff to work with us, and try to do more videos with other people and artists. We've got other long-term goals that we don't want to talk about yet, but hopefully those long term goals won't be as far off as we're expecting...

Among everything that the two of you have done on EYK, of what are you most proud?
I don't think we can use the word "proud" for anything that we've done. We're doing what we're doing because it's fun, and we're constantly amazed that anyone is having fun watching our videos as well. It's never a sense of pride as much as it's a sense of wonder and appreciation. We're most appreciative of the support we get from people and the wonderful comments they leave. It makes us all emotional far too often!

In what countries is EYK most popular?
We're viewed in 197 different countries, with 40 percent of our traffic coming from the US, 9 percent from Canada, 5 percent from Australia, and then 4 percent from Korea and Singapore.

Left to right
A woman wearing *hanbok*; a bell at Sanbanggulsa temple, Jeju Island. **Top** Fans of EYK in Mexico.

PART 5
SOCIETY AND
DAILY LIFE

South Korea is a land of contrasts. It is now a "cool" country, and one benefiting from a "Gangnam Style" image makeover. But it is also the most rapidly aging nation in the world. People in the West worry about the North Korean threat, but Seoul is also one of the safest big cities to live in. And despite the old "hermit kingdom" nickname, Korea is now on the way to becoming a multicultural society.

HOW KOREA IS CHANGING: IS KOREA XENOPHOBIC?

Many people ask me if I think Korea is a xenophobic or overly-nationalistic place, where foreigners are not wanted. Ten years ago, I would have probably said "yes"—but thankfully, things have changed a great deal in recent years. When I first arrived in Seoul older people (usually old men) would sometimes stare at me on the Metro with angry eyes. This doesn't happen any more, and in fact, I feel very welcome in Korea nowadays.

To be honest, one's treatment in Korea depends on where one comes from. A white Westerner will probably have very little trouble living in Korea today, but those from Southeast Asia in particular do tend to face discrimination. As with Mexicans in the US, people from Vietnam, Cambodia, Bangladesh, and so on are often stereotyped as poor, menial workers, and looked down upon by Koreans. This would suggest to me that the old race-based xenophobia is giving way to a new kind of prejudice—one based on economic status above all else.

Korea is fast becoming a multicultural society though, whether everyone likes it or not. Today, over ten percent of marriages have one foreign partner. This is driven by a growing open-mindedness from younger and middle-aged people, as well as the fact that men in rural Korea find it hard to attract wives—thus creating demand for mail-order brides from poorer Asian countries. And now, mixed race children are becoming popular in school, and are considered to grow up into physically attractive adults.

Above Faces of multiculturalism

Left International marriages now account for a tenth of all marriages.

Above Daniel Henney is a half-Korean, half-British celebrity. His popularity is symbolic of changing attitudes to mixed-race people in Korea.

THE PURE BLOOD IDEA

For many years, Koreans believed that they possessed "pure blood," never to be mixed with non-Korean stock. This idea arose in response to the Japanese occupation of Korea (1910–1945). Japanese authorities attempted to convince Koreans that they were a subset of the Japanese race; so, Korean historians came up with their own opposing theory—all Koreans were descended from a single, 5,000–year long unbroken bloodline, they said. It was not true, of course: throughout the entire history of Korea, there was mixing with Chinese, Mongols, Japanese, and people from even further afield. But the theory suited the times—colonialism made Koreans feel a need to preserve their sense of identity and uniqueness.

After independence and division, pure blood theory was adopted as policy by governments in both North and South Korea, and even taught in schools. President Park Chung-hee himself found it very useful in encouraging citizens to unite and participate in his plans for industrialization. Unfortunately, it also encouraged prejudice against any Korean who dared to date a foreigner.

Konglish on T-shirts is a very common phenomenon. I hope it never disappears!

Do You Speak Konglish?

One day while walking along the street near Pusan National University, I heard the enthusiastic voice of a random stranger shouting at me. "Do you speak English? I don't! I speak Konglish!"

What is Konglish? Like "Chinglish" in China and "Singlish" in Singapore, Konglish is the often charming hybrid that results from the combining of English with the local language. Koreans are exposed to English all the time, on television, in advertising, in pop songs, and so on, so it is no surprise that there are many opportunities for Konglish phrases and words to develop.

Occasionally the authorities start campaigns to eradicate Konglish. I also occasionally hear native English speakers in Korea complaining about why more isn't done to stamp it out. In my view, Konglish is quirky and unique, and an antidote to so-called standard English. I hope it sticks around.

A KONGLISH PRIMER
Without further ado, here are some of my favorite examples of Konglish:

A-S After-service. If your electrical appliances break down in Korea, the maker will fix them for free at an A-S Center.

BRAVO YOUR LIFE! This comes from an advertising campaign. Similar to "good for you!" or "way to go!"

BURBERRY MAN Amusingly, a Burberry Man is a public flasher.

CIDER Lemon soda. If a little kid tells you "I like drinking cider," don't be too alarmed.

CONSENT Plug socket or electrical outlet.

Dutch-pay "Going Dutch" and splitting the bill.

Fighting! You can do it!

GIPS A plaster cast. "Gips" is derived from "gypsum."

GLAMOR STYLE This describes a woman with large breasts. As in, "She's really glamor style!"

HANDPHONE Cellphone, mobile phone.

LEPORTS A combination of "leisure" and "sports."

LONG-DARI/SHORT-DARI Long-legged and short-legged. *Dari* is Korean for "leg."

NAME CARD Business card.

OVEREAT This doesn't mean "overeat" in Korea. It actually means "to vomit"!

JEONJA RANGE "Range" comes from "gas range." *Jeonja* is Korean for "electronic," so a *jeonja* range is, perhaps logically, a microwave oven.

MISSY An attractive older woman.

ONE-ROOM A small studio apartment.

S-LINE The curvy shape of a gorgeous woman's body is an "S-line." Like "Bravo Your Life," this one also comes from advertising.

SELCA Short for "self-camera"— a "selfie."

Service Anything given for no charge—such as a free beer in a bar, because the owner likes you.

SKINSHIP Touchy-feeliness.

TALENT a TV star. As in, "Lee Hyo-ri is my favorite talent."

EAT UNTIL YOUR BELLY EXPLODES: SOME GREAT KOREAN DISHES TO TRY

The Korean government puts a great deal of money into promoting Korean food around the world. Unfortunately, they go about it in the wrong way, emphasizing "relatively bland royal court cuisine and other foods that everyday Koreans rarely, if ever, eat," according to Joe McPherson, founder of excellent food blog ZenKimchi.com. Since Joe knows Korean food about as well as anyone—Koreans included—I asked him what dishes he would recommend instead. Here are his top four:

Dakgalbi Despite the cliche that foreigners "can't eat spicy food," this red pepper sauce-based chicken stew is a big hit with visitors to Korea. The home of *dakgalbi* is a lovely town named Chuncheon in the province of Gangwon-do; try spending a day there exploring temples like Cheongpyeong-sa and when you're done, go to the famed Dakgalbi Alley. As you can imagine, this is a back-street dedicated to the classic Korean dish.

Jjimdak More chicken stew, but this time with soy sauce and clear noodles mixed with carrots, potatoes, onions, and peppers. This is a very hearty dish, comfort food even. But it is also "fun and spicy," says Joe.

Boribap This is rural peasant fare, and is therefore precisely the opposite of the old royal cuisine the Korean government recommends you should eat. *Boribap* is basically just rice with barley, but you mix it in a bowl with a variety of vegetable *banchan* (side dishes) and *doenjang* (bean paste), and it tastes delicious. *Boribap* is all about simplicity, but with quality ingredients; Joe recommends a restaurant named San Maeul Boribap (in the town of Anyang, just outside Seoul) as having the best—as do I.

Godeungeo-gui Salted, grilled mackerel. This is a mainstay of *pojang macha* (roadside tent bars), where it is served as an accompaniment to *soju*. It's just a grilled fish, but dipped in a little soy sauce, it becomes heavenly. The historic town of Andong is a great place to try charcoal-grilled mackerel "with a perfectly crispy skin and moist, tasty flesh," says Joe.

Korean dishes worth trying. **Top** *Dakgalbi* **From left to right** *Jjimdak*, *Boribap*, and *Godeungeo-gui*.

Communal Dining

The real strength of the Korean dining experience is in the fact that everything—main dishes and side-dishes—is communal. Meat on a Korean barbecue, for instance, sits grilling away in the middle of the table, and anyone can jump in and take whatever they want, whenever they want. To me, it is an example of what I call Korea's "natural socialism." Nobody says, "You had more than I did," or "Don't eat that one, it's mine." And throughout the meal, everyone is constantly passing dishes, sauces, and drinks around the table, making for a very social, collective experience. It is a tasty meal on the one hand, but on the other, a bonding ritual and a distillation of Korea's culture of sharing.

Left and above The majority of Koreans like dogs as pets, and don't eat dog meat. But for those who are curious, this is what dog stew looks like.

Do All Koreans Eat Dog?

"Ah, you live in Korea. They all eat dog there, don't they?" This is a question I've been asked many times. I don't know why Korea takes all the rap for dog meat, when it is just one of many countries where dog is traditionally eaten. But the answer is, "Not really." Dog is by no means a popular meat, being nowhere near as commonly eaten as chicken, pork, or beef. That isn't to say that nobody eats it. Known as *boshintang,* dog soup can be found in backstreet restaurants in any town or city, as can *gaegogi suyuk*, or sliced dog meat. Both are eaten mostly by older men, who think that dog meat is good for their general health and "stamina." Stamina, in this case, is of the sexual variety.

"GREASY BEEF"
Having tried boshintang myself, I can't say it had any kind of effect on my, er, potency. The main impression it left on me was the taste, which I found to be rather like greasy beef. I can't say I enjoyed it. But frankly, I just wanted to try it for its exoticness, and didn't see anything wrong with eating dog—if I could eat a pig or a cow, why not a dog? Admittedly though, this logic is pretty much only accepted by older men in Korea. If I make the same argument to a young woman, I run the risk of being labeled a barbarian.

THE DARK SIDE OF DOG MEAT
Sadly, I later found out that the dogs are treated very cruelly—they are kept in tiny cages in places like Moran Market, Seoul, and killed by being beaten to death with sticks. This method apparently floods the meat with adrenaline, something which the old generation believes is good for—you've guessed it—stamina. So for that reason, I do not want to eat it again. That is of course not to say that chickens or pigs, for instance, are treated humanely either.

These days, there are plenty of anti-dog meat campaigners in Korea, including local members of PETA (People for the Ethical Treatment of Animals), who grab the headlines by engaging in naked street protests. Most young Koreans would agree with their view that what goes on at Moran Market is unacceptably cruel. When the subject of eating dog comes up, friends of mine will typically say that they tried it once or twice in their childhood days, with their parents or grandparents. It isn't something many of them go out and enjoy of their own accord.

Regional Specialities
As Joe McPherson often stresses on ZenKimchi.com, it is out in the countryside that the best Korean food can be found. The unique flavors of Jeju Island and the down-to-earth goodness of rural Gangwon-do need to be experienced, he says. The real breadbasket of Korea is the province of Jeolla-do. Jeonju, the most beautiful town in Jeolla, is famed for its royal connections as the ancestral home of the Yi dynasty—but it also has a number of unique local foods such as *galbi jeongol*, a pork rib stew. No matter where you are, try to wash your food down with regional liquors. Korea is rich in local brews and rural moonshine. *Makgeolli*—rice wine—is traditionally a farmer's drink, but is now popular with city yuppies, too, who are always seeking out new varieties from villages around the country. *Makgeolli* is best enjoyed with *jeon*, a kind of pancake. Then there is *soju*: if you're in Andong eating some mackerel, order some traditional Andong *soju* to go with it. This is nothing like the methylated mass-market stuff—it is strong, tasty booze that seems to heat up your whole body.

KIMCHI: IT AIN'T JUST CABBAGE

Kimchi is the most identifiably Korean thing in existence. It would be considered very strange to have a Korean meal without it. And for *halmoni-deul* (grandmothers), the ability to make good *kimchi* is a source of pride. Though you may simply think of it as spicy cabbage, *kimchi* is a cultural cornerstone, and as a food, surprisingly complex.

Believe it or not, there are around two hundred different types of *kimchi*. The "classic" cabbage *kimchi* is merely one of them. *Kimchi* can be made with radish, cucumber, and other types of vegetables as well, with all manner of seasonings added. *Kimchi* is basically a whole category of food—pickled vegetables—rather than one particular food.

Testament to the importance of *kimchi*, there is even a museum in Seoul dedicated to it. Those who wish to learn more about the finer points of pickled vegetables should therefore head to the Kimchi Field Museum for a full education in the history and preparation of this iconic dish.

KIMCHI SEASON

There is a traditional *kimchi*-making season named Kimjang, which falls in November, just ahead of the sub-zero temperatures that inevitably grip Korea in the winter. Markets are stocked full of cabbages, radishes, green onions, and other vegetables. Even in today's world of convenience stores and mega-marts where you can buy pre-made *kimchi*, many families go out to stock up on ingredients and make their own. Many older ladies in the countryside would consider it a shame to not make their own *kimchi*.

MAKING *KIMCHI*

How do those old ladies make it? Let's take typical cabbage *kimchi* as an example. The cabbage is cut up into pieces, and soaked in brine for a few hours. Getting the right concentration of salt is important, as too little makes the *kimchi* rot, and too much kills the bacteria needed for fermentation. The cabbage is then washed, and smothered in *gochujang*, a red pepper paste. The pepper paste can be bought, or made at home using red pepper flakes, fish sauce, ginger, garlic, scallions, and water. Making this paste is in itself an art

form—there are seemingly as many recipes as there are people, and everyone believes their grandmother's is the best.

The paste-covered cabbage is then placed in a jar, where it is left to ferment for a few days. The longer you leave it, the more sour the eventual taste will be. Then it needs to be stored. Traditionally, jars were buried in the ground in the winter, but today, many families have special *kimchi* refrigerators, which set the temperature just right. These fridges also enable people to store *kimchi* away from other foods—this is necessary as *kimchi* has a pungent smell that can easily contaminate anything in its proximity.

Top Readymade *gochujang* on sale in supermarkets. Plaster *gochujang* all over cabbage, and you have the basics of *kimchi*.

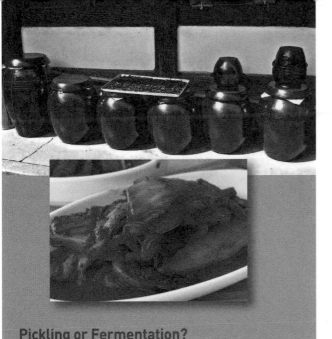

Gogi-jip: One of my favorite places to spend an evening in Korea.

Pickling or Fermentation?

The most important aspect of producing *kimchi* is fermentation. Koreans have fermented vegetables for centuries; chefs often say that fermentation is the "key" to Korean cuisine. Because the Korean climate is very extreme—boiling hot and sticky in the summer, and bone-dry cold in the winter—fermentation is needed to preserve vegetables to enjoy all year round. Korean chefs have also told me that fermentation is what makes *kimchi* "addictive." Fermented foods are said by some to have this property, with *kimchi* being no exception. Parents force their kids to eat *kimchi* when young, because it is socially important to eat it. But after the initial, "Ugh, that tastes weird!" they are hooked. The same was true for me. I didn't like *kimchi* when I first came to Korea, but now I eat tons of the stuff.

NAVIGATING THE *GOGI-JIP*

When the meat arrives, it will be uncooked. You grill it yourself at the table, so be sure to pay attention and turn the meat at regular intervals so that it doesn't burn. Scissors are also provided—these are for cutting the meat into bite-size chunks.

Meat is only a part of the meal. A whole range of side-dishes (collectively known as *banchan*), such as *kimchi*, assorted vegetables, garlic, peppers, and lettuce leaves, will also arrive. There will also be condiments such as *ssamjang* (a mix of pepper paste and bean paste), *chamgireum* (sesame oil), and soy sauce. One recommended way of eating a piece of meat is by dipping it in *ssamjang*, and then wrapping it in a lettuce leaf with some garlic.

To really fill your belly, order some *doenjang jjigae* and rice to go with your meal. *Doenjang jjigae* is a kind of soup made with bean paste, tofu, and vegetables. For me, the *gogi-jip* experience isn't complete without it. And don't forget to order beer and *soju* as well, if you are a drinker. Many people even drink *somaek*—a lethal mixture of the two—as they eat.

The *Gogi-jip*: A Korean Institution

If a group of Korean friends meets up, they will probably choose one of three places in which to get together—a coffee shop, a bar, or a *gogi-jip*. In one way, the *gogi-jip* is just a restaurant. But in another, it is also a social institution and national treasure.

Gogi-jip literally means "meat-house." When you go inside, you will notice a menu stuck up on the wall, offering various types of meat. The most popular choices include *samgyeopsal* (pork belly), and *galbi* (rib meat, either beef or pork). Prices are per serving, so for three people, you will want to order three servings to begin with, and then add more later if you are still hungry.

KOREA'S CHANGING POLITICAL LANDSCAPE

Everyone knows about South Korea's economic miracle. But it is also home to a political miracle. Since 1987, this country has graduated from military dictatorship to become one of the most vibrant democracies in Asia. But as with any democracy, politicians and their parties are not exactly beloved. Most people seem to consider their vote a choice of the lesser of several evils. But regardless, let's take a look at these choices.

THE SAENURI PARTY

Saenuri (formerly known as the Grand National Party) is the party of current President Park Geun-hye. She is the daughter of Park Chung-hee, the man who took control in a military coup in 1961, and kick-started the *chaebol*-led "economic miracle." Saenuri is essentially the descendant of his old Democratic Republican Party. Its big support base is in the province of Gyeongsang, especially in the city of Daegu—Park's hometown.

Because of the Park Chung-hee lineage, Saenuri is considered the party of economic growth and big business. It is also by far the most successful party, as it has provided four out of six presidents in the democratic era. It is a well-organized, well-funded, slick organization. Even when voters got tired of the *chaebols* and growing economic inequality in 2012, leader Park Geun-hye moved Saenuri to the center, and pulled off canny victories in both the parliamentary and presidential elections.

Park Geun-hye lost out in the race to be presidential nominee in 2007, to the man who went on to win—former President Lee Myung-bak. The two led their own factions within Saenuri, but as time passed, now-President Park gained the upper hand. Top party people like assembly leader Lee Han-koo are Park loyalists. And even after a year in power, Park's approval rating hovers around 60 percent, an unusually high figure.

THE DEMOCRATIC UNITED PARTY

This is the party that grew out of the opposition to military dictatorship. It is mainly composed of former democratization activists and old followers of the late former President Kim Dae-jung, the so-called "Korean Mandela." The DUP is strongest in the province of Jeolla, a part of the country known for its tradition of protest and left-wing politics.

The DUP has provided two presidents—Kim Dae-jung and Roh Moo-hyun. They almost made it three in 2012, but candidate Moon Jae-in—a long-time friend and confidant of Roh—ended up taking 48 percent of the vote compared to Park Geun-hye's 51. The party is considered left-wing due to its reconciliatory policy toward North Korea, and the fact that for many years, anyone who opposed the military government was painted as a communist. By the standards of most Western countries, it is basically centrist.

Many people tell me "I want to like the DUP, but I can't." The main reason for this is that the DUP is riven with infighting, has its fair share of corruption, and still seems stuck in the protest era. They only seem to show interest in opposing, rather than improving things: one disappointed party insider tells me: "Our strategists think that the way to win is just by attacking Saenuri."

AHN CHEOL-SOO

The DUP is now in serious trouble. A moderately progressive-minded businessman, Ahn Cheol-soo, won a seat in parliament as an independent in April 2013, and is now putting together his own party. According to opinion polls, an Ahn party would instantly become more popular than the DUP. Only time will tell...

Below A Saenuri banner thanking voters after Park Geun-hye was elected eighteenth president of the Republic of Korea in December 2012.

Below right Saenuri Party headquarters, Yeouido (Seoul).

국민여러분 감사합니다
국민행복시대를 열겠습니다

제18대 대통령 당선인 박근혜

THE UNITED PROGRESSIVE PARTY

The UPP is a left-wing party whose leader Lee Jeong-hee strongly aligns with trade unions, and wants to break up the power of the *chaebols*. She is also far too friendly toward North Korea for most voters. In fact, another UPP member of the National Assembly, Lee Seok-gi, is on trial at the time of writing for allegedly plotting to help North Korea in the event of an outbreak of hostilities between the two sides. The Korean government is now trying to dissolve the party, a move which is itself controversial.

THE JUSTICE PARTY

This is a progressive party that campaigns on workers' rights, gender equality, the environment, and so on. Its best-known politicians are Sim Sang-jeong and Roh Hoe-chan, who are both long-time left-of-center campaigners. Roh was a member of the National Assembly, but lost his seat in 2013. Why? He revealed the transcripts of secretly-recorded conversations showing corruption involving Samsung and politicians, prosecutors, and other officials. In doing so, he was deemed to have broken the law on communications, and was stripped of his right to sit in the assembly—a more serious punishment than any given to those involved in the corruption. There is also one notable wild-card independent. The funniest politician in Korea, Heo

Kyung-young, believes he has an IQ of 400, and claims to have spoken to the ghost of Michael Jackson. He is in no danger of winning anything, but did garner 100,000 votes in the 2007 presidential election—mostly from people who couldn't stand any of the serious candidates.

Above, from left to right Lee Jeong-hee of the UPP, Korea's most famous firebrand leftist; the author interviewing Moon Jae-in, defeated candidate in the 2012 Presidential election; and Heo Kyung-young, who claims to have met Michael Jackson's ghost!

Bottom left Roh Hoe-chan and Sim Sang-jeong of the Justice Party speaking against then-president Lee Myung-bak during the beef protests of summer 2008.

Below Members of the Democratic Labor Party (a forerunner of the UPP), protesting against the presence of the US military in Korea.

KOREA IS GROWING OLDER

Japan is famous for its aging population problem. But Korea is fast catching up. By 2050, Korea will be the "oldest country in the world," according to UN projections. By then, the average citizen will be 56 years of age.

The extent of Korea's *goryeonghwa* (aging) problem is easy to spot in everyday life. When I first started riding on the Seoul Metro, old people would use specially-provided seating in the corners of each carriage. Everyone else would sit in the middle. But now, the middle section is also full of retirees. And when I visit the countryside, I sometimes struggle to see young people at all.

Top left A group of elderly gentlemen hang out at Tapgol Park, downtown Seoul. Regular visitors will notice that "gray Korea" is now becoming a reality.

WHAT AGING MEANS FOR KOREA

The baby-boomers will be retiring soon. They will need their pensions and healthcare costs paying. But there won't be enough young working people to take care of it, because of the low birth rate. This will become a big drag on the economy. And an aging society is also one lacking in dynamism and creativity, as Japan has already discovered.

For those with money to invest, though, "Gray Korea" is an interesting trend. While an aging population is not good for the economy, companies that provide healthcare services, or insurance and pensions, will find big opportunities in Korea in the coming years. There will also be strong growth in the number of people moving back to the countryside, so picturesque villages should become boom-towns.

Korean politics is being affected, too. As in most countries, old people are more right-wing, and young people more left-wing. In the 2012 presidential election, there were more over-fifties voting than under-forties for the first time in Korean history. This was a big factor in conservative candidate Park Geun-hye's victory. In the future, Korean progressives will have to fight hard to win anything.

Baby Boom, Baby Bust

Back in 1960, the average Korean woman would have six children over the course of her life. As in other poor societies, people were accustomed to having large families. The economy started to take off, and with that, survival rates rose too. The result was a population boom.

Back in the 1980s and 1990s, this was good for Korea. A country with lots of young people—especially hard-working, educated ones like Korea had—is able to generate higher economic growth, other things being equal. But the baby-boomers themselves didn't end up having so many children. And now, the average birth rate is just 1.2 children per woman, around the lowest in the world. Mainly because of competition in education, parents believe they have to send their kids to expensive after-school institutes; this makes having an extra child too costly for most couples.

SUICIDE IN KOREA

Many people ask me why a country famous for its economic growth and pop culture explosion is in fact so unhappy. In my opinion, the main reason for this is a combination of two factors: competition and *chemyeon* (face). We saw how competitive Korean society is in Part One, but what is *chemyeon*? In Korea, as in other East Asian countries, there is an emphasis on showing good face. One needs to be seen living up to society's definition of success. In Confucian-based societies, one's social standing is of huge importance. In Korea, failing to meet society's expectations can result in tremendous anxiety and depression.

Just a few generations ago, the vast majority of Koreans lived in villages. Modernity has given Korea a lot, but many lament the loss of the closeness that this older, more traditional way of life gave them.

UNHAPPY RETIREES

Korea also has very high rates of suicide among the elderly as well. The younger generations have grown up as urbanites, as a direct result of post-1961 economic development. Older people originally came from the countryside, and grew up in very close-knit communities. But these days it is becoming more and more common for old people to feel abandoned by their relatives in the big city, and, since they are unlikely to know their neighbors, they cannot help but feel lonely. Added to this is the fact that Korea has one of the highest rates of retiree poverty in the industrialized world (almost 50 percent). So even in old age, the pressure does not let up.

The Tragedy of Suicide

For me, Korea is a wonderful country. I enjoy my work here, and have plenty of friends. But unfortunately, there are plenty of people who feel very differently. Every year, 31.7 out of 100,000 Koreans kill themselves. This is the highest national rate of suicide in the world. And the problem seems to be getting worse. According to a December 2012 survey in the *Chosun Ilbo* newspaper, 9.1 percent of Koreans had considered suicide that year. That is up from 7.7 percent just two years before.

Too Much Success?

Unfortunately, Korean society tends to define success very narrowly. A successful person is basically one who graduates from a respected university (such as Seoul National, Korea, Yonsei, or an elite American college), and either establishes him or herself in academia or public service, or makes big money in law, banking, medicine, or joins a well-known firm like Samsung. The only other people considered successes are extreme outliers, such as top athletes and movie stars.

Because there is so much parental and social pressure to fit this model of success, there are countless people living lives they do not want to lead. It is quite rare that an arty schoolboy will be encouraged by his parents to

pursue his passion rather than take a degree in, say, business or economics. And added to this, Korea's culture of hyper-competition makes it extremely hard for people even to squeeze into that strait-jacket of success. Because almost everyone wants to go to Seoul National University and then work for a "respected" company, demand far outstrips supply.

Hwang Sang-min, a psychology professor at Yonsei University, tells me that Korea is full of people following a dream that isn't theirs—and furthermore, competition means they can't even attain that dream. And because of *chemyeon*, he says, the failure to attain it results in a sense of great shame. People try as hard as they can to build up their public image, he says, but when they can no longer maintain that image, severe depression can result. He claims this is the main reason why Korea has such a high suicide rate.

Korea University—one of the "big three" institutions—along with Seoul National and Yonsei, are known as "SKY."

DOES KOREA HAVE CRIME?

Korea isn't a hundred percent safe, but it is one of the few countries I've been to where I'd feel perfectly relaxed about walking home alone late at night. Even the "rough" areas of Seoul are infinitely less dangerous than my hometown, a place where just 20,000 people live. The only time I have ever been the victim of anything remotely resembling a crime in Korea is when a drunken old man slapped my face (in a pitifully weak fashion) at a railroad station!

One reason for the general lack of macho violence in Korea is the fact that indulging in it costs money. If someone hits you first—and gets caught—they will most likely end up having to pay you the equivalent of several thousand US dollars. Thus it is common to see men squaring up to each other in bars or in the street, talking tough, but never throwing a single punch. The trick apparently is to make sure there are enough people around who will hold you back, making you seem like a tough guy as you raise your fist in an obvious fashion.

As in any country, I wouldn't suggest a woman or child walk home alone late at night. There is a certain amount of sex crime, and unfortunately, its rate of incidence has been increasing in the past few years. This, plus a series of notorious murder cases, has bred a climate of insecurity in the 21st century. Newspapers now run regular stories about sex offenders and murderers, heightening the sense of fear among the public.

THE NAUGHTY FORTIES

Interesting from a sociological perspective is the fact that crime in Korea is more likely to be committed by the middle-aged than the young. Forty-somethings are responsible for more crime than any other age group. Why is this? I have a couple of ideas: first, older Koreans grew up in tougher times, and thus tend to have a more aggressive outlook than the young. Meanwhile, there is a great focus on family unity in Korea, and when a young member of a family does something wrong, he is made to feel great shame over harming the good name of the rest. The fear of

shame, I believe, keeps a lot of young people on the straight and narrow. But because of age-based hierarchy, older people feel a little more emboldened to do whatever they want.

KOREAN GANGSTERS

I am sometimes asked whether Korea has large organized crime rings like the Yakuza of Japan. The answer is that Korea does of course have gangs—such as the *Chilseong-pa* of Busan—but they are not nearly so powerful as their Japanese counterparts. Gangs do dominate prostitution and loan-sharking, and provide muscle for construction companies seeking to evict residents standing in the way of redevelopment projects. Their heyday was during the 1950s, when President Syngman Rhee relied on *kkangpae* (gangsters) to maintain power. Their political influence today is quite limited.

I once had a night out with a *kkangpae*. He had apparently been a low-level hood who took the rap for a stabbing a boss had committed. After doing the time for this *hyungnim* ("big brother"), he was rewarded with his own swanky karaoke bar in an expensive part of Seoul. He was about as tall as me, but twice as wide, and with a handshake that I thought would crush my metacarpals. He seemed like a perfectly nice fellow—but certainly not one I would ever want to cross.

POPULAR MYTHS ABOUT KOREA

South Koreans live in constant fear of the North. American soldiers nicknamed Seoul "the killbox" thanks to the huge amount of rocketry North Korea has pointing at it. However, people living in Seoul never think for a moment about war. Any attack would mean instant retaliation and the destruction of North Korea. And besides, Seoulites have other things to worry about on a daily basis—money, relationships, and their health, for instance—just like everyone else in the world.

All Koreans want reunification. Generally speaking, the older generation believes very strongly that North and South Korea should be reunified. But those in their twenties, thirties, and forties tend to be a lot more skeptical. They were born after the division, and so have no memories of a united Korea. And the cost of bringing North Korea in line with Southern economic standards would likely cost over a trillion US dollars. "I don't want to pay for that," is a common response.

Korean food is "too spicy." For some reason, many Koreans believe their food is too spicy for anyone other than Koreans to handle. This claim is repeated very frequently in newspapers, on TV, the Internet, and in face-to-face conversation; thus, many foreigners end up taking it as fact. However, while Korean food can be spicy, it isn't always so. And as a matter of personal experience, Indian, Sichuan Chinese, and Thai food are more likely to blow my head off.

Koreans are poor. In 2011, I was telling a family friend back in England about *soju*. When I said a bottle of it cost around US$1 in convenience stores, he answered, "That's probably quite a lot for most Koreans, right?" South Korea has a GDP per capita (by purchasing power parity) of over US$30,000, and yet, the image of Korea in the West is still tied to the Korean War, M*A*S*H, and poverty.

Not everyone is into K-pop. Not everyone is worried about North Korea. And not all Korean food is going to blow your head off with an overload of red chili pepper.

All Koreans love America. And equally, all Koreans hate America. South Korea has been firmly in the United States's orbit since the end of World War II. Usually the older and more right-wing love Uncle Sam, whilst the younger and more left-wing think him an imperialist. However, what is true about attitudes to the US in Korea is that nobody ignores the land of the Stars and Stripes.

Everyone loves K-pop. K-pop is a big part of the Korean image abroad. But in Korea itself, there are a lot of people who can't stand the sugar-coated sounds of the nation's ubiquitous girl and boy groups. Meanwhile, there is quite a strong indie music subculture, and there are also many who love classical music, traditional Korean music, jazz, Western rock music, hip hop, and so on.

PART 6

KOREANS AT WORK

The Korean workplace is notorious for its long hours and rigid hierarchy. I experienced it myself, and didn't much enjoy it. But corporate Korea has also achieved more than its fair share of miracles. Fifty years ago, sweatshop workers made wigs; today, GDP per capita is close to Western European levels and corporate Korea churns out semiconductors and smartphones. Let's take a closer look at the Korean workplace...

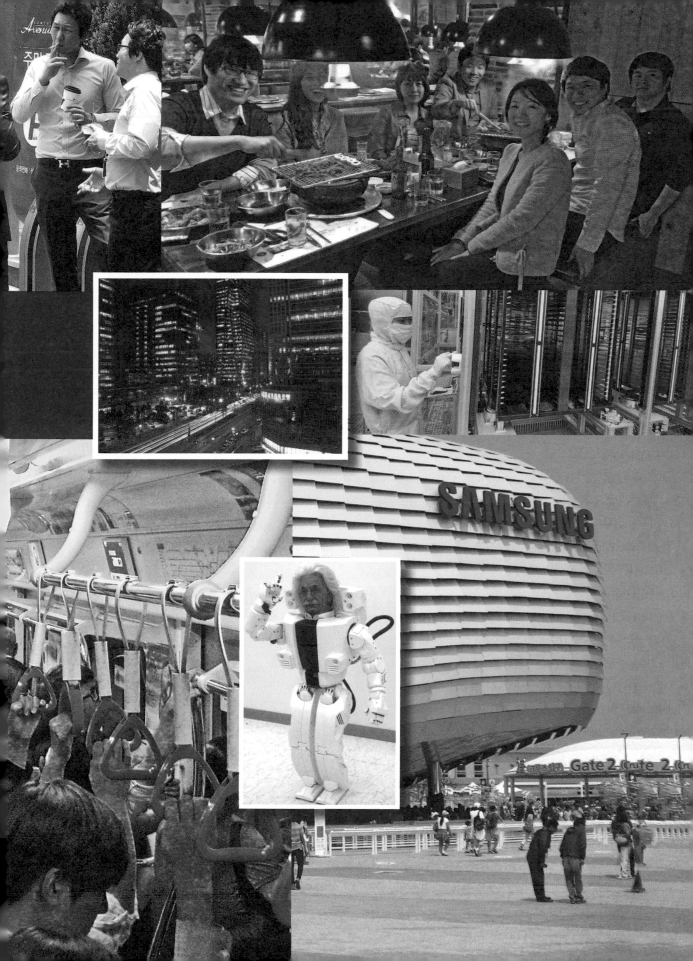

WORK FOR A *CHAEBOL*? NOT ME!

If you ask a Korean father, "What job would you like your son to have?" chances are he will say "lawyer," "doctor," or possibly even "civil servant." He also may say, "Anything at Samsung." These solid, stable choices are a reflection of Korean people's low tolerance for risk. Korea has not been a wealthy country for long, so people can still remember the times when a decent, secure income was the greatest blessing imaginable. Entrepreneurship is also a tough calling in Korea. *Chaebols* dominate almost every industry worth dominating, and it takes a brave or foolish individual to go toe-to-toe with one.

As a result, the biggest companies, like Samsung, have an abundance of applicants for every new job they create. They even set their own recruitment exams, like the "Samsung SAT," for which study guides are available in all Korean bookshops. Other things being equal, a man with a Samsung business card will have better social prospects, and better opportunities for marriage.

But these days, there is a growing band of youngsters who are not so interested in an ordinary, stable life, and who want to do something for themselves.

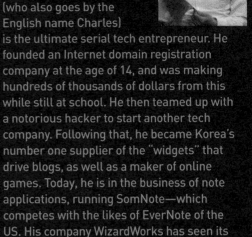

WizardWorks and Pyo Chul-min

My friend Pyo Chul-min (who also goes by the English name Charles) is the ultimate serial tech entrepreneur. He founded an Internet domain registration company at the age of 14, and was making hundreds of thousands of dollars from this while still at school. He then teamed up with a notorious hacker to start another tech company. Following that, he became Korea's number one supplier of the "widgets" that drive blogs, as well as a maker of online games. Today, he is in the business of note applications, running SomNote—which competes with the likes of EverNote of the US. His company WizardWorks has seen its share of ups and downs, but Chul-min's status in Korea as one of the most legendary young entrepreneurs is already secure.

REVENGE OF THE GEEKS

Several factors are driving this trend towards young entrepreneurship. The most important is that there are now a number of role models, such as the founders of great success stories like NHN (owner of the naver.com portal) and KakaoTalk, an instant messaging app used by 70 million people. Many of these founders are now re-investing in the next generation of start-ups, along with an increasing number of venture capitalists from Silicon Valley, Japan, and beyond. And with graduates of technology-focused universities like KAIST considered to be top-quality programers, there is a good pool of talent to justify their enthusiasm.

The government, concerned as it is about youth unemployment, is also getting behind start-ups in a big way. In 2012, one venture capital investor told me that "the government provides about 60 percent of the money" that Korean start-ups receive. This creates its own problems: how would the civil servant in charge of doling that money out know what a good business plan looked like?

But this question is of little concern to the army of geeks now setting up their own firms with that money. The most popular areas of activity are mobile gaming, and smartphone app creation in general. There are apparently 2,000 mobile game startups in Korea today.

Only a tiny fraction will make it. But those who do will themselves become role models, strengthening the culture of entrepreneurship and encouraging future generations of Korean techies to forget about the *chaebols* and do their own thing.

YOUNG TECH REBELS

Choi Jae-seung (Richard Choi), for instance—a twenty-something with an international school and American university background that would be the envy of most Koreans—has decided to start his own tech business, Spoqa. Spoqa operates Dodo, a loyalty points system that rewards users for visiting participating cafes and restaurants, and runs via a smartphone app.

As in Silicon Valley, Mr. Choi put together a team, and pitched his idea to venture capital investors. Quickly, one "angel" investor developed enough enthusiasm to fund Spoqa, and with that, he was in business. He still has work to do to convince older people that he is doing the right thing: "They look at my business card and say 'What's this?'" But those around his age admire him "for doing something nobody else is doing," he says.

Choi Jae-seung (Richard Choi), founder of Spoqa/Dodo.

WHAT IS A *CHAEBOL*?

Have you visited Korea and wondered why it is that a single company is able to sell you a trip on their coach, duty free goods in one of their stores, and a chocolate bar as a quick snack on the way back to the hotel that they also own?

The answer is "Park Chung-hee." President Park was the military strongman who ruled Korea from 1961–1979, and who divided Korean industry up amongst an elite club of insiders. He saw the impact that *zaibatsu* conglomerates like Mitsubishi had on turning Japan into a rapid-growth industrial powerhouse, and decided that this was what Korea needed, too. So instead of having a proper free market, company X was told to make cement, ships, and food, while company Y would make electronic goods and clothes, for instance. This was all conducted in accordance with a succession of "five year plans" introduced by Park himself. Over time, the companies best able to fulfil Park's demands were able to expand into a whole range of industries, and dominate them with his blessing. They became true conglomerates.

The closest Korean word to "conglomerate" is "*chaebol*" (a more literal meaning of *chaebol* is "financial clique"). In spoken Korean, however, another word is often used to describe them: *daegieop*, which just means "big business."

President Park lent the *chaebols* money at low rates of interest, and gave them government contracts, providing they did exactly what he wanted. Daewoo, which is most famous in the West for making cars, is also one of the world's largest shipbuilders—but not by choice. Founder Kim Woo-choong only entered the shipbuilding industry because President Park forced him to. Meanwhile, those who weren't part of the club found it virtually impossible to grow at all, because all the attractive markets were already occupied by Park-selected companies.

Over the years, several *chaebols* have come and gone. Daewoo itself went bankrupt in 1999, in the wake of the Asian financial crisis. Today, a definite hierarchy of *chaebols* exists, and a few top dogs have emerged. Some you will definitely know, and others you might not. Who are the kingpin *chaebols*, then?

The Big Five *Chaebols*

Samsung is the biggest of all, due to their flagship Samsung Electronics, responsible for the top-selling Galaxy phone. The group has gigantic influence over politics and the media. But did you know that Samsung can also sell you an apartment, a ticket to their theme park, and a 155mm howitzer artillery gun?

Lotte may not be as big as Samsung, but it is almost as ubiquitous. This consumer-focused *chaebol* produces all manner of snacks and drinks, and operates supermarkets, builds apartments, and sells insurance. You can also pay for all of these with your Lotte credit card.

Hyundai founder Jeong Ju-young grew up dirt poor in present-day North Korea. He famously stole the family cow and sold it, to provide him with enough money to get to Seoul and make his fortune. Today, his children run firms that make cars and ships, operate department stores, and construct buildings all over the world.

LG is an amalgamation of two old brands, Lucky and Goldstar. The former was known for producing household necessities like toothpaste, while Goldstar focused on electronics, making the first Korean radio. Today, LG still makes these products, as well as air conditioners, refrigerators, and televisions. Believe it or not, LG is also a major player in the fashion industry.

SK is unusual among big *chaebol*s in that it is not so well-known abroad. But it dominates some very important markets at home: SK started out making fibers, but now operates one of the country's largest mobile phone networks, produces chemicals, and is a major player in the oil and energy sector.

A HIGH-TECH POWERHOUSE: NEW, NEWER, NEWEST

Back in the 1960s, Korean products had one basic advantage. They were dirt cheap. With trade unions banned and GDP per capita sitting somewhere around US$100, nobody could produce textiles, wigs, and other low-tech items at a better price.

But from the early days of economic take-off under Park Chung-hee, big *chaebol* firms were encouraged to move up the value chain, making ever more advanced products for export. President Park instituted a succession of five-year plans, through which Korea progressively moved into more complex industries like shipbuilding, petrochemicals, and car manufacturing.

The spirit of the Park days was of constant change and the embracing of all that was newer, quicker, and technically superior. That mentality prevails, even today. Korean firms are no longer under so much government influence, but they remain paranoid about being left behind technologically. Samsung chairman Lee Kun-hee is known to tell workers that they should live in constant fear of being overtaken. And the general public, too, is always keen to trade up to the latest smartphone, "Smart TV," or super-fast broadband offering.

The result is that 21st century Korea is a kind of geek heaven. In London, you cannot get a phone signal on the Underground—but on the Seoul Metro, you can even access Wi-Fi and watch TV (also via your phone), if you want to. And did you know that in 1998—five years before Skype came along—a Korean firm was running an Internet telephony service, DialPad?

Central Park apartments, Songdo

SONGDO: KOREA'S TECH CAPITAL

The new, purpose-built city of Songdo is a hotspot of geek-dom in Korea. Like most big things in this country, Songdo is the product of co-operation between the government and *chaebols*. The state, along with steelmaker Posco and other large firms, is spending US$40 billion on constructing this so-called "ubiquitous city of the future." The whole of Songdo is served by free Wi-Fi. The top of the North-East Trade Tower has thermal imaging equipment that can detect fires anywhere in the city, and alert the emergency services. Even traffic lights are "intelligent"—sensors detect where cars are, and control the flow of traffic in the most efficient way, rather than using timers. Residents are able to switch on their heating by smartphone, so their apartment will be warm when they get back from work.

Why is Songdo a "ubiquitous city"? "Ubiquitous" here sounds like an example of Konglish, but actually it refers to the joining up of all information systems within a city through wireless networking or RFID tags, to make everything run more efficiently—from traffic flows to emergency rescue and power consumption. There are plans for 15 such cities in Korea.

Above An LG semiconductor factory. It is amazing to think that back in the early 1960s, Korea could compete in no industry more advanced than the manufacture of wigs.

Secret Stash

Korean women take care of household finances. Even a hot-shot fund manager will probably hand over his salary to his wife every month, and in return, she will give him an "allowance." Many women take advantage of this practice to build up hidden stashes—the advert here even offers a "secret savings" account for wives.

Far left Women of the Joseon Dynasty. Left President Park Geun-hye, in discussion with US President Barack Obama.

THE RISE OF KOREAN WOMAN POWER?

South Korean women only earn 63 percent of what South Korean men do. And according to the UN, the country is ranked only the 68th best out of 108 surveyed in terms of "empowerment" for women. Such facts are unusual for rich democracies. But then, Korea was ruled by the seriously Confucian Joseon Dynasty for over 500 years—ingraining sexism into the psyche of the nation. During the later Joseon era, it was not considered proper for a woman to be involved in public life at all.

When Park Geun-hye was elected President on December 19th, 2012, conservative Korean newspapers implied it was an historic moment for women. But Ms. Park is no ordinary woman. She is the daughter of Park Chung-hee, the military strongman who built modern South Korea. And her cabinet is, as expected, full of men (nineteen out of twenty, to be precise).

The *Ajumma* Brigade

You will find very few women high up the ladder in Korean business or politics. However, in a way, ladies like these (pictured) are the driving force behind Korea's economy. If you go to any market or supermarket, you will see working-class *ajumma* (middle-aged women) and *halmeoni* (grandmothers) busting their guts to pay for their kids' tuition fees, wedding expenses, and so on.

IT'S MAN'S WORLD

Back in 2005–2006, I worked in the Korean investment industry. The first place I worked was small, and had no female staff. The second was a big fund management firm, but despite having hundreds of executives, I don't remember ever seeing a single high-ranking woman. There were plenty of smart young women lower down the ranks, but it was customary for them to leave after marriage.

This was not entirely the company's fault. Traditionally, husbands wanted to be the provider. I have worked with women with masters degrees in statistics who now do nothing more complicated than taking care of the kids and making *doenjang jjigae*. Their husbands considered it a point of pride that their wives didn't work. The growing cost of raising children, though, means this mentality is starting to change...

More Women in the Workplace

As always with Korea, things are changing fast. It is only seven years since my time as a "salaryman" in Seoul, but I can see how young women now are finding opportunities even their older sisters might not have had.

It is hard to believe, but a majority of new appointees both to the judiciary and the elite stream of the civil service, are female. Many foreign firms in Seoul have taken advantage of *chaebol* sexism to scoop up smart young female talent. And big Korean firms themselves are finally starting to change, hiring and promoting women in greater numbers.

It is the younger generation who are open-minded. A boss in his fifties may still think of his wife as "her indoors," but an up-and-coming thirty-year old man will probably want a well-educated wife with an income of her own. Today's young women, then, are much more likely to keep working. And when they break through into executive positions, Korea's gender pay gap will start to diminish substantially. In 2013, Korea finally got its first female bank CEO, Kwon Seon-joo of Industrial Bank of Korea.

Yi Soyeon (Korea's first astronaut) once told me that her mother missed out on school, because her family didn't believe that girls should be educated. She then went on to discuss her own life: "When I was studying for my PhD, old professors would say, 'Oh, your work is pretty good for a woman,' and constantly refer to me as a 'female engineer.' But my male peers just saw me as one of the group, no different to them." That tells you that things are starting to change.

THE IMF CRISIS OF 1997–98

South Korea in the 1980s was a country on the way up. The economy was flying, free and fair elections were finally achieved (in 1987), and the whole nation felt justifiably proud of hosting the 1988 Seoul Olympics. In under three decades, the transformation from basket case to miracle country had been seemingly completed. But a hidden time-bomb lay ticking...

Right Trade union protestors. Below Ex-President Lee Myung-bak (front row, second right) at a conference on the world economy.

A NATION IN CRISIS

The Korean economic miracle was built mostly on struggle and hard work. But it was also partly built on debt. Large *chaebols* had been borrowing huge amounts of money from government-owned banks for years. They expanded recklessly, safe in the knowledge that even if they lost money, they would always be able to borrow more. During the Park era, government officials encouraged as much borrowing as possible, as it was customary for them to receive kickbacks on every loan.

Things finally came to a head in November 1997. Several *chaebols* were already in trouble by that point, with Kia Motors requiring emergency loans that July. But the trigger for total chaos came when the Thai baht collapsed, spreading fear throughout East Asia. Investors panicked, and fled Korean assets. The Korean won went from 800 per US dollar to 1700 almost overnight. Since the nation had borrowed dollars from foreigners, the cost of making repayments effectively doubled. Soon, it wasn't just the *chaebols*, but the whole country that was in trouble.

THE IMF BAILOUT

South Korea turned to the International Monetary Fund (IMF) for a bailout. The IMF forced the government, businesses, and trade unions to accept corporate restructuring (and job losses), high interest rates, and a dramatic liberalization of rules on foreign capital that made many Koreans believe they had lost their economic sovereignty. For this reason, the crisis is still referred to by most Koreans as the "IMF Crisis," even though its root cause was rampant *chaebol* debt addiction. Those three letters, IMF, are still remembered with

bitterness in Korea. Many will talk of that time as a period of humiliation. It is also a time that brings to mind store-fronts with "IMF Sale!" and "IMF Discount!" signs—i.e., last-ditch efforts to head off bankruptcy.

PATRIOTIC GOLD

Surprisingly, one of the most famous stories of the "IMF Crisis" era was a positive one. In January 1998, the Korean government announced it had collected 660 lbs (300 kg) of gold, sent in by members of the public. People donated it in order to save their country's economy—since the central bank had no reserves, the idea was to melt down the gold, sell it, and use the money to rebuild. Sadly, Koreans only held enough gold to cover a third of the US$58 billion owed to the IMF, but psychologically, it was a very powerful symbol of national unity. South Korea

is a very divided country, but in times of trouble, people are able to pull together.

LASTING DAMAGE

Korea did quickly re-emerge from the crisis and went back into rapid growth mode. But psychologically, the impact of 1997–98 crisis is still being felt. Korean workers had not been used to layoffs: there was an unspoken agreement between worker and company that years of devotion would be rewarded with job security. In an instant, that was all gone. Korean workers are no longer especially loyal to their firms, and their firms no longer feel such a need to take care of their workers.

The crisis also naturally caused increases in depression and suicide, as well as the divorce rate and incidence of domestic violence. Many Koreans still talk about the "IMF" period as the most tumultuous, terrifying period they can remember.

IMF-led labor market liberalization also meant the start of a new era of irregular work. In the wake of the crisis, firms stopped offering as many "regular" jobs and instead started turning to temporary contract workers, interns, and part-timers, all of whom are much easier to get rid of than normal employees. In the fifteen years that followed, their numbers rose to the point where one third of all workers were irregulars with poor salaries, prospects, and job security.

"880,000 WON GENERATION"

Many of the irregular workers mentioned above are on or near the minimum wage, which is currently 5,210 won (around US$5) per hour. In a country where a cup of coffee costs around the same amount, such a sum does not go far. Those unlucky enough to be caught in this trap are known as the "880,000 Won Generation," so named after the amount they are able to take home in a month.

WAITING FOR A CHANCE

You would be surprised at how well-educated many of the 880,000 Won Generation are. In Korea, around four in five young people will enter university; the BA degree is treated as a baseline minimum rather than an achievement. But there aren't enough good jobs available for all of those graduates. Those who fail to make it will likely end up in low-paid *bijeonggyujik,* or irregular work.

Such twenty-somethings have grown up believing that education is their ticket to prosperity. Their parents forced them to study hard in school, with the understanding that they would be rewarded later. But instead, they earn the minimum wage in convenience stores and restaurants, whilst hoping for the day when their thousandth application for a "proper" job results in success. Education mania and high aspirations were great for Korea in the beginning—but now they are double-edged swords.

> **When I hired a *bijeonggyujik* worker...**
> I saw the extent of the *bijeonggyujik* problem when I put out an advert on a website asking for a Korean teacher. I asked applicants to contact me with a suggested hourly rate. To my surprise, I awoke the next day to a deluge of e-mails offering lessons at prices as low as 5,000 won (around US$5) per hour. I eventually chose one of them— a graduate of the well-respected Sungkyunkwan University—and ended up offering her fifty percent more just to stop myself from feeling guilty. It was still a bargain price.

THE PRESSURE NEVER ENDS

Youngsters aren't the only ones who have it rough. There is also the issue of forced early retirement. Men in their fifties are also usually supporting university-age sons and daughters, exacerbating the problem. Because they are pushed out of their high-paying jobs, they are forced to make ends meet by driving taxis, or working as security guards, for instance. Those with savings can open small businesses, such as restaurants or cafes—but even these fields are dominated by *chaebols*, so it is hard to make a decent living. Many open fried chicken and beer shops (see page 92)—it has become common to see *chicken-hof ajosshi* slaving away over frying machines, in sadly empty bars. One security guard in my building used to make a decent living at a respectable company. But now he earns the minimum wage—as does his wife, who works in a supermarket. They have some savings, but he says they will not last much longer. His state pension will not kick in for several years, and in the meantime, he will have to continue to support his family. He hopes that his children can avoid joining the 880,000 won club, so they can take care of him in his old age.

Clockwise from top left A part-time casual laborer puts up posters. Union members protest against job cuts. A middle-aged *ajumma* works in a supermarket.

ARE YOU *GAP* OR *EUL*?

Two of the most important words to know when it comes to business and daily life in Korea are *Gap* and *Eul*. These are two short words with a very long history. They represent the first two of the ten so-called "heavenly stems" from a day-counting system that originated in Shang Dynasty China over 3,000 years ago. That system is a relic, but *Gap* and *Eul* survived, and came to be used in legal contracts to define two parties, in the manner of "Mr. A" and "Ms. B." They have also taken on a very powerful extra meaning in spoken Korean.

A QUESTION OF STATUS

So what is that extra meaning? Simply, any person with the upper hand in a relationship is *Gap*. The one who has to submit to *Gap*'s whims is *Eul*. If you have a boss, he is definitely *Gap*. If you run a shop, your customer is *Gap*. And if you run a small firm supplying nuts and bolts to Samsung Electronics, you are *Eul*—though you will be *Gap* to your employees.

The *Insa*
When you meet someone for the first time and exchange words of introduction (*insa*), you should bow. Unlike in Japan, however, there is no specific angle at which you must bow. Simply saying a few polite words and lowering your head should suffice. Then you may shake hands and exchange business cards.

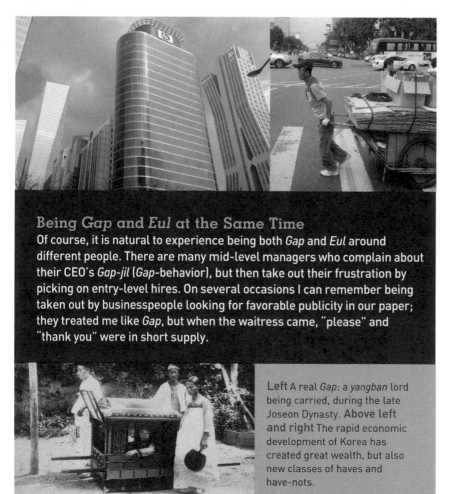

Being *Gap* and *Eul* at the Same Time
Of course, it is natural to experience being both *Gap* and *Eul* around different people. There are many mid-level managers who complain about their CEO's *Gap-jil* (*Gap*-behavior), but then take out their frustration by picking on entry-level hires. On several occasions I can remember being taken out by businesspeople looking for favorable publicity in our paper; they treated me like *Gap*, but when the waitress came, "please" and "thank you" were in short supply.

Left A real *Gap*: a *yangban* lord being carried, during the late Joseon Dynasty. Above left and right The rapid economic development of Korea has created great wealth, but also new classes of haves and have-nots.

Because of Korea's history of strict social hierarchy (which derives from Confucianism), it is unfortunately common for those in the *Gap* position to abuse their status. At one Korean company I worked for, the chairman regularly rounded up female employees and made them go drinking with him, even though they obviously didn't want to. And it is quite normal to see shop customers talking down to cashiers, using the most impolite form of Korean.

In 2013, *Gap* and *Eul* relations became a red-hot conversation topic, thanks to a series of well-publicized incidents. In one case, a director at POSCO, one of Korea's largest firms, hit an air stewardess for apparently not preparing a pot of instant noodles in the "correct" manner. In another, a manager at milk supplier, Namyang Dairy, was recorded swearing at and talking down to a franchisee (in Korea, franchisees are definitely *Eul*, and the main firm is *Gap*). These cases enraged the public, at least partly because they reminded the average citizen of their own experiences of being *Eul* at work.

Jeong Ju-young and Hyundai

Since the beginning of Korean industrialization, Hyundai and Samsung have duked it out for the right to be called number one *chaebol*. Thanks to the astonishing success of its mobile phones, semiconductors, and televisions, Samsung is currently top dog. But in a way, Hyundai is the more iconic of the two companies, due to the personal story of its founder, Jeong Ju-young.

HUMBLE BEGINNINGS

As mentioned above, Jeong was born into rural poverty. His family were subsistence farmers. After arriving in Seoul in 1933 at the age of eighteen, he did a variety of manual jobs before going to work at a rice store. The owner saw Jeong's dedication and talent for business, and decided to hand the shop over to the young man upon retirement. This happened when Jeong was just twenty-two years old.

Jeong ran the rice business well for two years, before the Japanese colonial authorities forced him to shut it down. In those days, there were very few industries in which Koreans (other than collaborators) could operate without Japanese interference. He turned his attention to one such area: vehicle repair. He eventually went on to open Hyundai Auto Service in 1946. This turned out to be a wise move, as the incoming US Army had a lot of trucks that needed regular maintenance.

Jeong then used his reputation with the US Army to gain construction contracts during the Korean War of 1950–53. His building arm, Hyundai Engineering and Construction, prospered throughout the war but nearly went bankrupt a few years later, due to the unexpectedly loss-making Goryeong Bridge project. This ended up costing Jeong 70 million won (a huge sum in those days). But in fulfilling the contract in spite of the trouble it caused him, the government came to trust Hyundai. Hyundai soon recovered and went on to become the country's top construction firm.

Below One of Hyundai's gigantic container ships, built at Ulsan. **Right** Jeong Ju-young.

Park and Jeong

Park Chung-hee came to power in 1961. Angered at the corrupt relationships that existed between the previous administration and the business community, he rounded up the most prominent entrepreneurs and even paraded some through the streets with placards saying, "I am a corrupt swine." But soon, he realized that he could use their organizational skills to help industrialize the country. Jeong, along with Samsung founder Lee Byung-chul, became his favorites. Park believed they were the most talented, and so directed great amounts of state money and contracts towards them. This cemented the position of Jeong Ju-young and Hyundai at the top of the Korean business world.

With Park's help, Jeong went on to a number of extraordinary achievements. He built the world's largest shipyard in the southeastern city of Ulsan. And in 1975, Hyundai Motors produced the Pony, the first proper automobile developed and built in Korea.

He also used his very limited free time to become a noted womanizer. Not long before his death in 2001, a journalist asked him if he was still able to satisfy his coterie of lovers as he used to, despite his advanced years. His reply was, "Well, not at the same time."

WORKPLACE DRINKING RITUALS

Another part of Korean *wolgeupjaengi* ("salaryman") life I experienced during my time at an investment firm was the *hwaishik,* a late night, after-work drinking session. The consumption of large amounts of alcohol with co-workers is the main way in which team-members bond in Korea. In Korea, it is a great advantage to one's business career if one is able to drink well. And if you can sing well at the *noraebang* afterwards, you'll do even better...

HWAISHIK SESSIONS

Sometime during the day, a team head will announce, "Ok everyone, let's go out tonight." Only the very best excuse can get you out of this. Most Korean workers will have had the experience of having to cancel an appointment with their friends at short notice, in order to appease the boss's demand for a drinking session. When work ends, all members of the group will head to a restaurant—"Korean barbecue" (*samgyeopsal* or *galbi* for instance) would be a good place to kick off the proceedings—and start drinking with their meal. Typically, they will have beer or *soju.* Those who can't handle their alcohol may even be quite drunk by the time they leave the restaurant. Once the meal is finished, it is time for *I-cha,* the "second round."

I-CHA: THE SECONG ROUND

I-cha will be at some sort of bar. If the company is doing particularly well, this may mean an upscale place, but typically, it means a *chicken-hof.* *Chicken-hof* is an absolute institution in Korea, where cheap local beers such as Hite or Cass are served along with fried chicken. These places can be independent, or part of chains like 2:2 Chicken, Chicken Baengi, or Gubne Chicken (Gubne actually bake their chicken rather than fry it, for the benefit of the more health-conscious beer-guzzler).

At the *chicken-hof, soju* and beer will likely be mixed together to make a lethal drink called *so-maek* (this word combines *soju* and *maekju,* the Korean word for beer). You should drink this in one go, with team members shouting

The main ingredients of a *hwaishik*—clockwise from below: A neon *noraebang* sign; co-workers around the barbecue table; a bottle of *soju*; fried chicken; *samgyeopsal* ready to go on the grill.

"One shot!" as you do so. By around 11 PM or so, everyone will be pretty drunk. At this point, it is time to go to the *noraebang,* or singing room.

SAM-CHA: THE THIRD ROUND

Everyone gets their turn to select their favorite song from a machine, and blast the eardrums of their co-workers. Those who are not singing will either dance, or shake tambourines (these are also provided). *Noraebang* lasts around one hour, and when it is over, everyone goes home—or, in the case of more macho offices, the women go home, and the men pretend to. Men may then slyly reconvene around the corner, and head on to a "room salon" (a kind of hostess bar), if business is going well enough to pay for it. I have had *hwaishik* evenings that went on until 4 AM. Sadly, this did

not mean I could take the next morning off. Work started at 8 AM as normal—though nothing would actually get done (small wonder, then, that worker productivity in Korea is second-lowest in the OECD). All team members would sit around groaning "never again," and reaching for special hangover remedy drinks like Yeomyeong-808 or Condition (see page 98). But "never again" was, of course, a lie. We would do this roughly twice a month. At other firms, twice a week was more like the average. No surprise, then, that per capita deaths from liver cirrhosis have risen ten-fold in the past thirty years.

YOU'RE NOBODY WITHOUT A BUSINESS CARD

In Britain, most people I meet do not bother handing me their business card. Plenty do not even have business cards. In Korea, though, virtually everyone will have a stack ready for every time they make new acquaintances. And it isn't just workers: very often, students will have their own cards with their university logo on top.

WHY ARE BUSINESS CARDS SO IMPORTANT?

As with other Confucian-influenced countries, Korean culture tends to place great importance upon a person's position within society. That position is mostly determined by their place of work (or study), and the rank they hold there. When you meet someone in Korea for the first time, chances are they will want to "size you up" in this way, so they will hand you their business card, in expectation of receiving yours.

When I first arrived in Seoul, I worked as an English teacher. Fairly or not, foreign English teachers are not really respected in Korea. But when I joined an investment firm as an equity trader—and started handing out my new card—I instantly felt the difference. People would openly say, "Wow! I assumed you were *just an English teacher*," and take approving second and third looks at my card. It was all extremely superficial of course, but I cannot deny that it opened doors for me.

THE ETIQUETTE OF EXCHANGING CARDS

Since business cards are important, there is a certain amount of etiquette surrounding their exchange. Like any object handed over in Korea, one should give and receive business cards with two hands. But after receiving one, you should also take a lengthy look at it, and preferably offer some sort of approving comment. Only then you may put it away in your pocket, but even then you should do so with care rather than with a quick, careless motion.

Then, you should hand over your card—the other person should treat your card with the same respect you showed his/hers. Since even Seoul—a city of ten million—often feels like a village, you may then be asked "Ah, you work for such-and-such company! Do you know [Mr. or Ms. X]?" If you've been around a while, the answer will probably be "yes." Having mutual friends and acquaintances is of course useful anywhere, but even more so in Korea. People thus put great effort into broadening their networks.

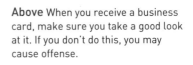

Above When you receive a business card, make sure you take a good look at it. If you don't do this, you may cause offense.

A small part of the author's gigantic business card collection. If you live in Korea, you'll accumulate masses of them.

Do I Use *Hangeul* or *Hanja*?

Korean business cards are usually very conservative in terms of design, except for those of people in the creative industries. Most contain two sides of text, with one written in Korean, and the other, English. And if a person is of very high status—a CEO, a government minister, the chief editor of a newspaper, and so on—they will usually switch Korean *hangeul* for Chinese *hanja* characters, as *hanja* is considered sophisticated. Not all Koreans can read *hanja* well though, so there is something undeniably elitist about this custom.

한글
漢字

PART 7 KOREANS AT PLAY

Koreans work longer hours than people in any other developed country. But that doesn't mean they don't know how to enjoy themselves—Korea is in fact a place that really likes to party. Let's take a look at a few of the ways in which Koreans cut loose.

HOW TO BE A POLITE "ALCOHOL WHALE"

In English, a fellow who loves his booze is said to "drink like a fish." In Korea, he would be a *sul-gorae*, or "alcohol whale." And with the highest rates of alcohol consumption in Asia, it is hard to deny that Korea is a good country in which to be one.

Why is this? My best guess would be that Korea's love of alcohol could have something to do with the freezing cold winter weather, the historic lack of a religion that forbade drinking, the stressfulness of living in a hyper-competitive country, and the presence of *han* and *heung*. But whatever the truth, Korea today is a country in which young and old, rich and poor, male and female—all enjoy a tipple without any social stigma.

ANJU TIDBITS

Having been to a British university, I can be quite an enthusiastic *sul-gorae* myself. But although Brits and Koreans have an equal love of drinking, the way in which they consume it is different. The first thing the visitor should learn is that there is no drinking in Korea without food. Unless you go to a Western-style bar, you will be expected to order *anju*—food made to go with your drink.

Popular *anju* include fried chicken, which people usually enjoy with beer; *jeon*, a kind of pancake that goes well with *makgeolli* (rice wine); and grilled fish, which helps those punishing *soju* shots go down. Korean bars will typically have a wide selection of *anju*, so there should be at least one thing that appeals to your taste buds.

YEOGI-YO! MORE DRINKS!

In a Korean pub, one does not go up to the bar to order. Instead, drinkers summon the waiter's attention either by shouting "*yeogi-yo*!" ("over here!"), or pressing a button attached to the table. I love the button; some places even have separate buttons for beer and *soju*. And unlike where I come from, there are no "rounds." You simply pay for everything at the end. "Going Dutch" is usually frowned upon as well. Over the course of an evening, you will probably visit several different bars, so if your friend takes care of the bill at the first establishment, you should pick up the tab at the next one.

WHAT TO DRINK?

The average Korean night out will involve a lot of beer, or a lot of *soju*. Or both. Western liquor is also popular, especially whisky, the drink favored by businesspeople. Korea is now the world's fifth largest importer of scotch, with brands like Johnnie Walker and Ballantine's doing great business here.

Above A "take-out" bar selling cocktails in plastic pouches. **Left top** Koreans enjoying *soju* with grilled fish at a *pojang macha* (street restaurant). **Left lower** *Jeon*, popular *anju* for rice wine (*makgeolli*).

Drinking Etiquette

Probably the most useful thing of all to know is the etiquette of pouring drinks. If you have bottles of anything—beer, *soju*, whisky, and so on—don't just serve yourself while letting your companion's glass go empty. Take the bottle and pour theirs first, using two hands. Then hand the bottle to them, and hold out your glass—also with two hands. Your friend will then pour for you.

Then clink glasses before you drink. You will probably find yourself saying cheers a lot more in Korea than in the West. All Koreans know the word "cheers," but to do it properly, say "*keonbae*." There are other words that serve the same purpose, though. *Jan* is the simplest; then there is the enthusiastic *wi-hayo!*, which means "to us."

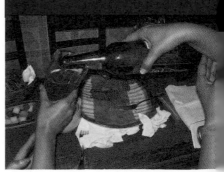

The Joys and Sorrows of *Soju*

Korea has a strong tradition of native liquors. The most common is undoubtedly *soju*—the little green bottles of main brands Cheoeum Cheoreom and Chamiseul are a ubiquitous presence in every *gogi-jip* and *pojang macha* up and down the land. Chamiseul is actually the world's most popular spirit in terms of quantity sold, though its cheap price (1,300 won per bottle in a convenience store, or about 4,000 won in a restaurant) means it is certainly not the most lucrative. In a sense, such commercial *sojus* are not the "real thing"—they have a taste that is bland and chemical-like in comparison to the excellent traditional *sojus* made in places like Andong, a town in Gyeongsang province. These are made from starches like rice or potato. I'm not exactly sure what goes into mass-market *soju*, and I don't think I want to know!

MAKGEOLLI RICE WINE

Other than *soju*, the most popular drink has to be *makgeolli*, which is usually referred to as rice wine in English, but is closer to beer in terms of its alcohol content. *Makgeolli* is milky white in color, and very refreshing in taste—though one must admit, the prospect of a makgeolli hangover is not one to be taken lightly.

Until recently, *makgeolli* was considered country bumpkin booze, being as it was cheap and made by rice farmers. City folk rarely drank it. I finished my first stint living in Korea in 2007, and returned in 2010; in those three years, *makgeolli* had somehow gone from zero to hero. I am not sure why this happened, but it could have something to do with *makgeolli* being relatively low in calories, or having a "natural" image because of its farm origins. As is the case in other wealthy countries, Korea is now falling in love with all things organic.

There are as many kinds of *makgeolli* as there are towns in Korea. Though there are big companies making it, small regional brewers claim a big portion of the market. As with craft beer, there can be great variations in flavor; I have had nutty *makgeolli*, and even strawberry-flavored *makgeolli*.

Far left
Makgeolli (rice wine) served in the typical fashion.

Left A bottle of Jangsu *makgeolli*, one of the most common brands available.

OTHER DRINKS TO TRY

Cheongju This is another rice-based spirit, clear in color, and somewhat similar to Japanese sake in taste.
Insamju "Insam" means ginseng; *Insamju* then is believed to be healthy and drunk as a medicinal spirit.
Baekseju Rice is brewed and infused with a mixture of eleven herbs and ginseng. It also has a healthy image—*baekseju* actually means "hundred year life drink." Some people mix it with *soju*, though, to make *oshipseju*—"fifty year life drink"!
Sansachun This is a brand-name liquor, made from *sansa*, a kind of hawthorn.
Bokbunja is a kind of raspberry, which is used to produce a deep red-colored wine-like drink of about 15 percent strength. It has a powerfully fruity taste, and apparently is quite healthy, as far as alcohol goes.

Above If you go out to the countryside, you will find an array of local brews.

Baem-soju I have never had the pleasure myself, but it is still possible to find *baem-soju*. This is *soju*, but with a snake inside it!

POPULAR HANGOVER CURES

As we have already established, drinking is a very popular way to spend an evening in Korea. But what do you do when tomorrow comes and you don't have the option of just sleeping it off? A whole industry has sprung up to try and answer that age-old question. Go to any convenience store and you will find a choice of hangover cures in small glass bottles and cans. They sell for between 3,000–5,000 won, and most contain the extract of a plant named *heotgae*, which has been used to brighten up the morning after by East Asians for centuries.

Speaking from experience, I have to say that they work rather well. My concoction of choice is named Yeomyeong-808, a patented drink which I find reduces the aches and mental fogginess that can be expected after a night on the *soju*. Yeomyeong has made inventor Nam Jong-hyun a wealthy man; he also owns a Korean league football team, Gangwon FC.

Other popular remedies include Morning Care and Condition. One of my old bosses described the latter as a "miracle cure" after trying it on a business trip to Seoul. I keep wondering when someone will make a deal to export these to the rest of the world. If I ever become rich, I will do it myself.

Drink More, Study Less: Advert for a bar near Sogang University, in Seoul.

Yeomyeong-808 If you're feelng a little rough after a night on the *soju*, head to a convenience store and grab a can of this. It's not cheap, but it is pretty effective!

Urusa Bear's Bile

For hardcore drinkers, there are even daily pills which makers claim, boost your liver function—keeping you healthy as well as hangover-free. The most famous, Urusa, is supposedly made from the bile of bears. As cruel as that may sound, Urusa is very popular. In a 2012 survey almost half of Korean CEOs asked named Urusa as their favorite nutritional supplement.

HAEJANG-GUK HANGOVER SOUP

There are also foods that are considered good for hangovers. *Haejang-guk* is "hangover soup" and can be eaten as supper after a drinking session, or for breakfast or lunch the next day. *Haejang-guk* contains soybean paste, cabbage, scallions, and most notably, ox blood. There is also a variety *(Bbyeo-haejang-guk)* that contains pork on the bone, with clear noodles as well.

Haejang-guk

I find that any meaty soup or stew can do the job. Back when I lived in Gangnam, a friend and I would often finish an evening out with a bowl of *galbi-tang* (beef rib soup) at a well-known restaurant named Parkdaegamne (Master Park's Place). Even at four in the morning, the place was always busy.

Some also swear by *haejang-sul*, but not me. This means "alcohol to cure a hangover"—in other words, having a "hair of the dog." Yeomyeong and *galbi-tang* will always be my favored method.

THE TRADITIONAL KOREAN NIGHTCLUB (YES, REALLY)

Next to a small dancefloor, tables are laid out in seemingly endless rows. Patrons spend most of their time sitting there, rather than dancing. They order bottles of whisky and plates of fruit—and wait for something known as *"booking."* Booking is a practice whereby a a waiter approaches a table of women and leads them to a table of men, with the aim of them hitting it off.

In this way, each patron may meet ten or more different people over the course of the evening. In one sense, this type of speed-dating sounds like a conservative relic from a time when introductions were everything. But considering the number of one night stands that happen after booking, there is also something quite decadent about it.

Naturally, men like booking more than women, so the deal is sweetened for female patrons. Their entrance is cheap or even free, in contrast to the chaps, who must pay around US$100 or more per person to cover the whisky, table, and waiter's tips.

If the woman is disappointed with the man the waiter introduces, she will just get up and leave with barely a word said. But if an introduced pair take a shine to each other, it is customary for them to exchange phone numbers after about ten minutes of conversation. They may also go up to dance for a while, to music that can only be described as bad 90s techno.

CLUBBING IN KOREA

More up-to-date dance music can be found at "Western style" clubs in Gangnam, Hongdae, Itaewon, and other areas of Seoul where young people hang out. There has long been a heavy American musical influence on Korea, so US chart hip-hop dance clubs are very common; recently though European house music has become popular, and the most popular superclubs in Gangnam—Eden and Octagon, at the time of writing—mostly play that style. Though Seoul is not internationally famous for clubbing, big-name DJs like Tiesto have been known to come and play (for rather shocking ticket prices).

Though Seoul leads the way, Busan comes a close second. The area around Kyungsung University is a big party destination, as is the main downtown area of Seomyeon. And during the summer months, Haeundae (Korea's most famous beach resort) clubs come alive with visitors from all over the country. There are other party cities though, such as Daejeon. If you ever find yourself in Daejeon on a Friday or Saturday night, head to the Dunsan-dong district behind a department store named Timeworld for a guaranteed big night out.

Above The street behind the Hamilton Hotel, Itaewon (Seoul)—one of the most popular areas for a night out. **Below and top right** Female clubbers dressed in Hongdae Style and Gangnam Style, respectively (courtesy of Styleshare).

Itaewon

When I first visited Korea, Itaewon was treated as a no-go zone by most locals. It had a sleazy reputation as a place of prostitution for American servicemen. In the past few years though, Itaewon has become cool—mirroring the increased acceptance of foreign culture in Korea. Today, Itaewon is full of clubs, bars, and restaurants that draw huge crowds of Gangnam Koreans. Increasingly, foreigners are heading down the road to the Gyungridan district, where prices are a bit cheaper, and queues shorter.

THE *NORAEBANG* SONG ROOM

Those who have had their fill of beer, *baekseju*, or *bokbunja*, often find themselves going to a *noraebang*. This literally means "song room," and that is exactly what it is—a small room with a karaoke machine, couches, and a couple of tambourines. From my experience, it is the number one place to take out your stress in Korea, or just go a little crazy. *Noraebang* turns even the meekest people into would-be Ozzy Osbournes.

If you are in Korea and find yourself with the urge to sing, here are a few things you'll need to know.

1. First things first. There are *noraebang* places in absolutely every built-up area, so you won't have any trouble finding one. You do not need to make a reservation—simply enter, and pay the manager at the front desk. He will then point you to your room.

2. Cost. *Noraebang* is paid for by the hour, and should cost between 10,000–20,000 won for the whole room (not per person). One hour is usually enough for most people, and if the place isn't so busy, the manager might give you a little extra time for free at the end. And if you find yourself having too much fun, you can simply pay for an additional hour.

3. Refreshments. The vast majority are not licensed to serve alcohol. But some will sell you beer "under the table," if you ask nicely. There will also be a refrigerator stocked with soft drinks at the front desk. Snacks will be on sale, too.

4. Using the machine. The room will contain a thick book full of song titles and numbers. There will be a gigantic Korean section, large English and Japanese sections, and maybe even some Chinese and Philippine songs available. If you wanted to sing "Hey Jude," you would go to the English section, look up the song under the letter "H," and find a number next to it. Then, you would pick up the remote control, type in the number, and press the big green "start" button on the bottom right corner.

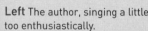

Left The author, singing a little too enthusiastically.

If you want to give up halfway through, there is also a "cancel" button on the bottom left. And if you want to reserve a song (for instance, your friend is singing "Hey Jude" and you want to do "Gangnam Style" next), type in the relevant number and then hit the "reserve" button in the bottom middle of the remote. "Gangnam Style" will then start automatically after "Hey Jude" is finished.

The remote control is quite complicated, as it has a number of advanced options. You can change the pitch to suit your own range, jump ahead to the next verse if there is a long instrumental break, or add echo. Most people do not use these functions very often, though.

5. Be a good *noraebang* partner. When others are singing, shake a tambourine, or even dance if you feel like it. Don't be a microphone hog—take it in turns! And if you pick a really long song, like "American Pie," remember that you don't need to sing the whole thing.

Finally, don't be too shocked when the machine awards you a score out of a hundred at the end of the song. Nobody takes these scores too seriously, and in any case, the number is usually generous. If your friend gets less than ninety, make sure to question the machine's judgment.

The DVD-room

The DVD-room is a private cinema for two. Much like the *noraebang*, DVD-rooms are found all over large cities, especially in areas popular with young people. The bar and restaurant-heavy Jongro area of downtown Seoul, for instance, is full of them.

To enjoy the DVD-room experience, one should take a significant other, and 10–15,000 won, to cover the cost of renting the movie. Upon entering the building, you will have a choice of hundreds of Korean and Western movies; subtitles are also available if you need them. After telling the manager which movie you want, you will be given a room number. Finding it will typically involve negotiating some dark corridors. Once you get inside, you will see a faux-leather couch, a big screen TV, and nothing else. Although intended for dating couples, there are also those who go to DVD-rooms alone, or with friends, simply to watch movies.

The DVD-room is in some way also a reflection of Korea's private *bang* (room) culture. Aside from *noraebang*, Korean cafes often have private sections for meetings. Fancy restaurants also have private rooms, in which you may find some CEO, politician, or celebrity holding court.

Bang: A Little Background

Back in the Joseon dynasty, a *yangban* lord would keep a special room in his house, named the *sarang-bang*. He would use the *sarang-bang* to entertain guests, typically other gentlemen with whom he wished to discuss politics or scholarly matters.

The *sarang-bang* usually also contained a study, named the *sarang-chae*. This was a private space for scholarly reflection, and one into which no woman was allowed.

The lady of the house also had her own room, named the *an-bang*, into which only family members were permitted to enter.

THE "DATE COURSE"

As with lovers the world over, Korean couples like to walk hand in hand through tree-lined streets and parks, without a care in the world. Back in the 1960s, when few people had any money and Korean social values were much more conservative, a romantic walk in the park was effectively a date in itself. In the old movie *Cho-woo*, the heroine tells her admirer to meet her in a park on the next rainy day. He jumps for joy when the rain finally comes down...

Today, a date will likely consist of a meal and coffee, and probably a romantic walk between the restaurant and the cafe. Altogether, this forms a "date course," a useful Konglish expression to know. In Seoul, good places to wander through on a date course include Cheonggyecheon, a restored stream that begins near City Hall and stretches on for around two miles (three km); Samcheong-dong, a tree-lined, winding road with all manner of cute little cafes and art galleries; and Seochon, a delightful neighborhood full of *hanok* houses, but without the traffic levels of Bukchon. If you happen to find yourself in Busan, go to Taejongdae—it offers dramatic cliffs and views of the sea. Whatever you do, make sure you avoid the palace, Deoksugung. Superstition has it that a couple taking a walk through its grounds will soon break up.

Above Tea for two at one of the many cafes in the district of Samcheong-dong.

SPORTS MANIA STRIKES

The "big three" sports in Korea are football (soccer), basketball, and baseball. The latter two are a direct result of American influence on Korea, while the first gained popularity in the wake of the 2002 World Cup. Schoolboys know how to play all three, and grow up admiring the likes of ex-Manchester United player Park Ji-sung, or the LA Dodgers' Ryu Hyun-jin. There are also professional leagues, with most teams being unsurprisingly owned by *chaebols*.

Korea is also full of gym hounds. Particularly in Seoul—a built up city full of very busy people—it makes more sense to hit the treadmill for half an hour before work rather than go out somewhere for a run. Gyms, yoga studios, pilates clubs and the like are everywhere. But much like the rest of the world, there are far more people who join than who actually do regular exercise. Those quick dropouts are guilty of *jakshim-samil* ("three days' determination").

Left Park Ji-sung is probably Korea's most successful footballer, having won the English Premier League and the Champions League with Manchester United. There is even a highway named after him in his home city of Suwon. Fans love him for his humility and the fact that he overcame adversity on the road to success—he has two flat feet!

THE LEGACY OF 2002

2002 created several heroes. Team captain Hong Myung-bo, whose cool defending kept out technically better teams like Portugal and Spain; Lee Woon-jae, the goalkeeper who faced Spain in a penalty shoot-out; and Ahn Jung-hwan, whose headed goal against Italy saw them through to the quarter-final. But the whole team shared in the legend: the government decreed all squad members to be exempt from military service. Many, like former Manchester United player Park Ji-sung, went on to play in European leagues. Long-haired Ahn Jung-hwan even became a kind of metrosexual heart throb, appearing in commercials for male cosmetics! Unfortunately, 2002 was the high point: the Korean team hasn't progressed be-

yond the last sixteen since then. But the fans' enthusiasm remains undimmed. If you want to join them in 2014, here are three proper nouns worth knowing:

The chant: "*Dae-han Min-guk*! (clap-clap-clap-clap-clap)." This is *the* chant. It just means "Republic of Korea" (the official name for the country), and though a simple chant by the standards of a British footy nut, it is addictive and easy to remember. In 2002, if you stood in any busy area and shouted it once, it would set off a street party. I can remember banging a drum to "*Dae-han Min-guk*!" and leading a procession of a dozen people around the student district of Hyehwa-dong.

The place: City Hall (Si-cheong in Korean). The circular lawn outside Seoul's City Hall building is ground zero for red devil fandom. Hundreds of thousands gather there even before the game, creating a carnival atmosphere. You'll see people dressed in the wackiest costumes, but with one style rule to guide them: wear red. There are also young women who attempt to "sex up" their outfits to get noticed. Every World Cup, one of them will become a star—such as Mina, who caught the attention of photographers and managed to turn her popularity into a singing career.

The legend: Guus Hiddink. Mr. Hiddink was the Dutch coach who guided Korea to the semi-finals in 2002. Despite not being Korean, he is possibly the living person most beloved by Koreans. In my opinion, he is part of the reason why Koreans are now much more open to foreigners. Every national coach since has suffered from being measured against his yardstick, and found wanting. Even today he remains one of the world's most sought-after coaches.

Hong Myung-bo Korea's captain in 2002, Mr. Hong is now manager of the national team.

The author, with Guus Hiddink

Red Devil Mania

Every four years, the FIFA World Cup comes around. And for as long as the Korean team stays in it, the nation grinds to a halt.

Even my own "Korea story" is deeply entwined with the World Cup of 2002. Korea hosted the event along with Japan, and luckily, a Korean friend of mine from university had some match tickets. A group of four of us came over, and had our minds blown by the experience. On match-days, literally everyone dressed in red, and millions congregated in places like City Hall (Seoul), or Haeundae Beach (Busan), to watch the "red devils" play on giant screens. Whenever Korea scored, the ground shook. After a victory, parties would go on all night. There was even a "World Cup baby" phenomenon.

CROSS MY PALM WITH WON

South Korea is an undoubtedly modern country. But ancient superstitions continue to have great influence over its people. As well as practitioners of shamanism, there are thousands of people working as fortune-tellers in booths, roadside tents, and special *saju* cafes up and down the land.

If you give the year, month, date, and time of your birth to a *saju* reader, she will use them to come to an understanding of your nature as a person, and how it relates to the world around you. Her analysis will be based on theory contained in the "Book of Changes" *(I Ching)*, an ancient Chinese text. She will then advise you on what may happen to you in the future, as well as how you ought to live.

A man providing all kinds of superstitious services in the Jongro area of Seoul. He offers baby naming, fortune-telling, and face-reading.

MY EXPERIENCE WITH *SAJU*

I received *saju* once in a cafe in Apgujeong, an expensive part of Gangnam in Seoul. My consultation cost just 5,000 won, though I hear that these days, it can cost about 9,000 or even 10,000 won. My friend and I ordered drinks, and waited for the fortune-teller to come. The place was busy, so we had to wait a while. Finally she sat down with us, and took my "four pillars" of destiny—year, month, date, and time of birth.

She took this information and consulted her book, all the while furrowing her brow as though in deep thought. Finally she wrote down eight Chinese characters (each of the four pillars has two corresponding characters), which together, are supposed to govern my nature.

She then interpreted what the characters meant for me. According to her, I am a flighty person, who ought to live in a hot country. She said there would be two women in my life. Most importantly of all, she told me that my life would be meaningless until I reached the age of 25 (I was 23 at the time), but thereafter, I would be a great example to others. I'm still waiting for this to happen, but I continue to hope!

DO YOU BELIEVE IN *SAJU*?

Most people would say that they do not really believe in *saju*, and that it is just a bit of fun. This is particularly true for young people. *Saju* can even be something for dating couples to do together, as opposed to just having a chat in a normal coffee shop. And many *saju* readers themselves see their work as just another job. They are not necessarily well-trained, and receive an unimpressive hourly wage. They may even offer tarot and Western-style fortune telling as sidelines.

On some level though, people are affected by *saju*, particularly when looking for some reassurance over a difficult situation. There are many older ladies who go to the fortune-teller quite regularly, particularly when they are faced with a problem or have a big decision to make. The mother of a friend of mine has a regular fortune-teller she visits, not in a cafe but in the fortune-teller's own home; this one charges more, is considered to give quality readings, and gets to know her clients in depth. My mother's friend is also a regular visitor to a shamanist *mudang*—people who believe in one are likely to believe in the other as well.

HEAD FOR THE HILLS!

Over 70 percent of land in Korea is mountainous. It is no surprise then that mountains have an important role in Korean culture. Shamanist *musok-in* revere them as gods, traditional art is full of cloudy peaks, and Baekdusan—the tallest mountain on the Korean peninsula—is as much a symbol to Koreans as Mount Fuji is to the Japanese.

In daily life though, the mountain is a place of leisure. Korea's favorite pastime is hiking. Popular routes at famous peaks like Hallasan (Jeju Island), Seoraksan in the east, and Jirisan in the south, sometimes become so busy on weekends and public holidays that hikers have to walk up in lines. This can be frustrating, but at least the view from the top will always be rewarding.

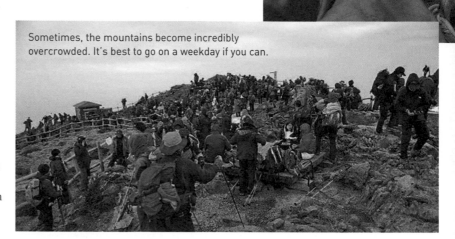

GRAY ON TOP

Older climbers in particular take their hiking very seriously. If you take the Seoul Metro early on a Saturday or Sunday morning, you will see large groups of senior citizens dressed in brightly-colored mountain gear, and kitted out with proper hiking boots, walking poles, and provisions for a long day ahead (though they are known to do this even when going up smaller hills). This is a sight you can see even on shockingly cold winter mornings.

Some old climbers are so healthy that they embarrass those half their age. I have often been overtaken on the way up by hikers in their sixties, who stride ahead with the aid of their spiky walking sticks. More than likely, they will also be pushing ahead under the power of *makgeolli*, rice wine. It is customary for hikers in Korea to take a little drink with them for the road.

Sometimes, the mountains become incredibly overcrowded. It's best to go on a weekday if you can.

Fallen leaves on the path down from Cheongnyangsa Temple, Cheongnyangsan Provincial Park, Bonghwa.

The Baekdu-daegan trail

The most enthusiastic trekkers should get out of Seoul and hike the Baekdu-daegan trail, the ultimate in Korean hiking experiences. The 930 mile (1500 km) Baekdu-daegan range forms the spine of the Korean peninsula, from Jirisan in the south all the way up to Baekdusan, which sits by the North Korea–China border. Politics means you can only do half of it, but that alone apparently takes two months. Those who would like to know more should check out Roger Shepherd and Andrew Douch's book, *Baekdu Daegan Trail: Hiking Korea's Mountain Spine.*

HIKING IN SEOUL

Seoul is a true megalopolis. But it is also built around mountains, making it a great city for a hike. If I walk for just half an hour from the busiest downtown area, I can look down upon the whole city. For me, the most enjoyable trek is up Bugaksan and the old Seoul Fortress walls, just to the north of Cheong wa Dae (the "Blue House"), the presidential mansion. It offers excellent views, but is also a hike rich in modern history.

In 1969, a team of North Korean commandos came over Bugaksan with the intention of assassinating president Park Chung-hee. They failed, but bullet holes in trees marking their shootout with South Korean forces remain even now. The area was made off limits to the public after the attack, but was thankfully reopened in 2006.

Other popular peaks around Seoul include Gwanaksan behind Seoul National University, and Bukhansan, which also gives its name to a national park. My favorite is Inwangsan, which also happens to be the most active site for shamanism in Korea.

SWEATING IT OUT: THE JJIMJILBANG AND SAUNA

One of the great Korean leisure institutions is the *jjimjilbang*. *Jjimjil* means bathing to treat the skin, but in practice, the *jjimjilbang* is so much more than that. Over the years, it has evolved into a kind of spa complex, in which you can bathe, take a sauna, sleep, have something to eat, and generally hang out with friends.

TIME TO GET NAKED

But lets talk about the bathing part first. After paying the entrance fee at the front desk and storing your shoes in a locker, take either the male or female door (depending on your gender, obviously). You will not then see a person of the opposite sex until you leave the baths. Why is this? The reason is that bathing is done completely naked.

The first time I went to a *jjimjilbang*, I must confess that I found this a deal-breaker. Nonchalantly stepping out in my birthday suit in front of complete strangers is something I am simply too British for. Added to this is the fact that I am a tall, hairy, foreigner, which tends to make some people stare out of curiosity. If you can get over such anxieties, grab a shower in the changing room, and head out into the bathing area.

Once inside, you will be greeted with a whole range of pools and jacuzzis in which to vegetate or reinvigorate yourself. Choose wisely, though—the 46 degrees celsius pools can provide a bit of a shock to the system at first. Lying around in one of the cooler pools first is the best way to start, and then if you feel ready for it, move up and boil yourself like a lobster. Then when you are done, why not take a sauna? Like the Finns, Koreans love relaxing in a steam room and sweating out the stresses and strains of everyday life.

MORE THAN JUST A SAUNA

After you're done bathing and sauna-ing, your body should be positively glowing. All of the awkward nakedness and heat will have been worth it. You can then head to the relaxation area (clothed, in regulation shorts and T-shirt provided at the front desk), where you can watch TV, or simply lie on a mat and fall asleep. Some places have exercise equipment, massage shops, and even *noraebang*. There will also be a refreshments area, where you can eat cup noodles, *patbingsu*—a dessert made of shaved ice and sugared bean— or a variety of other snacks.

One of the great advantages of *jjimjilbang* is the price. It should cost no more than 10,000 won (US$10); most charge less than that. It is thus a cheap and fun way to hang out with friends at the weekend. You can in fact spend as long as you like there—many people even sleep overnight in the *jjimjilbang* when they find themselves in another city, or when they need to recover from an excessive evening out. The *jjimjilbang* opens 24 hours a day, so no matter how late it may be, you will always be able to find a place to crash and fall asleep when you are in Korea.

Jjimjilbang is one of the most popular and relaxing ways to spend free time in Korea.

THE COMIC BOOK WORLD OF *MANHWA*

The whole world knows the Japanese word "manga." Few know its Korean equivalent, *manhwa*, which is derived from the same two Chinese characters. But Koreans are almost as enamored with comic books and graphic novels as their counterparts across the sea. There is even a museum dedicated to it in Seoul.

HOW SIMILAR IS *MANHWA* TO MANGA?

Just like manga, *manhwa* takes the reader into a fantasy world of characters with special powers, androgynous features, and ginormous eyes (the latter being an interesting cultural point: large eyes are considered desirable in East Asian countries). In fact, the Korean *manhwa* industry is greatly influenced by manga. Though Japanese cultural imports were banned until the late 1990s—a reaction to Japan's colonial rule of Korea—illicit manga books found their way into the country, and inspired a many a young artist.

Physically though, the books are bigger than in Japan, and content is read left to right, rather than right to left. A typical *manhwa* book will cost around 9–10,000 won if bought online, and a little more if bought at Kyobo or YP Books, the two largest book chains in Korea. A trip to Kyobo's main store in Gwanghwamun (downtown Seoul) will show you the extent of manhwa's popularity: huge sections are devoted to it, along with further sections for manga, either translated or in its original form.

As with manga, some of the most popular *manhwa* have also been translated into English. These include *Chocolat* (the tale of a boy band fan-girl who tries to scheme her way into meeting with her idols) by Shin Ji-sang; and *Bride of the Water God*, a more classic fantasy by Yun Mi-kyung. Yun Mi-kyung in particular is a very popular *manhwa* artist.

Above The first woodcut *manhwa*, by an unidentified artist, printed in 1908.

Top "Cosplay" isn't as popular as in Japan, but it does have its fans.

Hyung Min-woo, Korean *manhwa* artist demoes his drawing of "The Priest."

MANHWA-BANG

When I first arrived in Seoul, there were also little *manhwa-bang* rental shops in every neighborhood. Much like an old video rental shop, you could go there to borrow a comic book for a short time, for a small fee. Back then, I taught English at a language institute; several of our students were *manhwa* addicts, much to their parents' annoyance. They would spend lunch breaks in the *manhwa* shop, and would then come back to class and sneakily read the books they borrowed, under the covers of their English textbooks.

ONLINE *MANHWA* WEBTOONS

As with all creative industries, the Internet is shaking things up. The *manhwa-bang* is disappearing, and the consumption of "webtoons"—online *manhwa*—has become extremely popular. These are free, supported only by advertising; and because they are independently produced, they tend to have edgier themes (to see what I mean by this, look up the "Bongcheon-dong Ghost" webtoon, which is also available in English).

Webtoons are free to read, but that doesn't mean that they can't be commercially successful in the end: The story of one sea urchin boy, "Marine Blues," was a webtoon that first appeared in 2001, garnered millions of readers, and ended up being turned into physical books and computer games.

Wara Store This is a kids' TV cartoon, made by a good friend of mine. It is based on a webtoon, which first came out on the Naver portal in 2009.

Comic World Seoul

Comic World Seoul events are held once a month, and are a visual spectacle that bring Harajuku straight to mind. One online commentator notes that you can see "fox girls, robots, ghosts, Victorian couples, men from space, elves, Lolitas, and pixies" there. Make sure you either get a ticket in advance, or arrive early, though: queues can get very long.

Participants also sell homemade stickers and posters, featuring fan art of their favorite characters. Sometimes, this even extends to the non-anime world: K-pop fan art is also a big deal in Korea. You can also attend Comic World in Busan, where the event is held every two months, at the BEXCO conference center.

Details Comic World is held at the SETEC center in Seoul, near Hangnyeoul Station on Line 3 of the Seoul Metro. Entry is 4,000 won. Check www.comicw.co.kr for more information.

PART 8

KOREA'S
MUSIC SCENE

The Chinese used to consider the Koreans "the people dressed in white, who love singing and dancing." The clothing is now more varied, but the rest of the characterization still holds. Korea is mostly known for K-pop these days, but has some great independent music as well, and a fun native style of pop called *Bbongjjak*.

THE K-POP FACTORY

On one level, K-pop is just pop music made in Korea. But the word conjures up so much more than that. Think five, six, or even nine surgically-enhanced, heavily made-up boys or girls dancing in such tight formation that you might think they are being remotely controlled; super-slick production based on the latest trends in American pop, but with sometimes surprisingly wholesome lyrics about love; and everything overseen by an army of behind-the-scenes staff—managers, songwriters, choreographers, and marketing men—who leave nothing to chance in the quest to make the most desirable product possible.

They are very successful. K-pop dominates in Thailand, is big in Japan and China, and has started to make inroads in Latin America and Western countries as well. Korean boy bands like Shinee are able to fill 50,000-seat arenas in Tokyo. The biggest K-pop label, SM Entertainment, has seen its stock price rise *fifty-fold* in the past five years. Main rivals YG and JYP are also making big money.

How did they do it? In my opinion, they took the Japanese pop business model, and ran with it. That means taking very young (teenage or even pre-teen) wannabe stars and training them for endless hours in dancing, singing, and even foreign languages (for future world domination). It means strictly controlling their image, and signing them up to long contracts. The system began in the late 1990s, with the success of groups like SES, Shinhwa, and HOT. But that was just the beginning. Today's top performers like Super Junior, Big Bang, and Girls' Generation enjoy international stardom that their forebears could only dream of.

Psy and K-pop Psy is part of the YG Entertainment roster, but he isn't your average K-pop star. For more than a decade, he has been churning out tongue-in-cheek hits in Korea, like "Champion." He doesn't take himself at all seriously, and in a pop scene where nobody else is allowed to have a single hair out of place, he is a breath of fresh air.

INSIDE THE K-POP MACHINE—AN INTERVIEW WITH IDA SIMMONS, AMERICAN K-POP TRAINEE

To find out more about K-pop from the inside, I talked to Ida Simmons, a half-Korean native Californian who became the first Westerner to enter the K-pop factory as a trainee with SM Entertainment. They eventually placed her in a duo named Isak & Jiyeon, which released two albums but "fell through the cracks" on the way to stardom, she says. Here's what Ida had to say:

On the K-pop lifestyle: We lived in a dorm, like in college. There was a bunch of girls staying in each room. This was to save money, but also so they [the management] could keep tabs on you. We had no say in what music we wanted to do. But we had a nanny who cooked and cleaned, and bought groceries for us. But it was also tough. In the business, they want you to be mean and step on someone else. They would constantly tell me, "You're too nice!" They want to build a bit of rivalry between the girls.

You're only allowed to date after your second album. When one member of [boy band] Super Junior announced he had a girlfriend, that was a huge issue. You're held up to different standards. I got caught dating someone and they threatened to get rid of me. My partner in the group got caught as well, and we had our phones confiscated for a year. Really, they're investing in you as a product—you are a product, whether you like it or not.

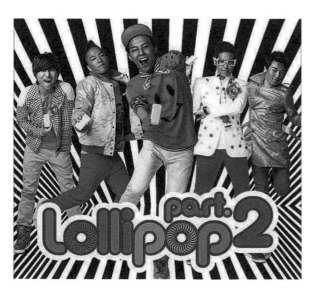

Girls' Generation are probably the most popular K-pop group of the 2010s. This nine-member singing and dancing powerhouse was launched by SM Entertainment in 2007, following on from the massive success of their boy band, Super Junior.

Below left The headquarters of SM Entertainment, one of the big three K-pop companies.

Balancing trainee life with school life: After school, we'd be dropped off at SM and stay there until 10, 11, or 12 midnight. And in school vacations, we'd be there at least 12 hours a day. If you want to sleep, sleep here, they'd say. A lot of Korean singers just give up school. But because we were doing it at such a young age, we felt privileged. There was a lot of jealousy at school.

Infamously long contracts: These days, they only sign for three years. But I spent twelve years with SM [until recently, contracts like this were normal]. Do I regret it? No! At the time, my dream was to be an entertainer. If you ask any entertainer in Korea, they'd say the same. You can't put a price on it.

The fraught path to stardom: At the beginning [because I was mixed-race] nobody thought I'd be marketable, except for [SM founder] Lee Su-man. Also, K-pop was changing a bit at the time. In the early 2000s, there was a big boy band boom, and then sentimental ballad singers came in. We were an R&B duo, so we fell through the cracks. But this is life, I'm not going to sulk over it. If I could turn back time, I wouldn't change it.

Getting to [huge boy band] TVXQ status is about a million to one chance. And 90 percent of these idol groups, what are they going to do ten years from now? But they keep doing it because they love it. Kids these days are starstruck by the idea of being a singer.

Do you know how many idol groups have debuted this year? It's about 80! If three succeeded, that would be a good figure.

Internal Politics: After our group broke up, I was frozen out for a year. I went to the SM building, and they said there's no room for you. I was kicked out of Korea for a while because my visa expired. Also, we weren't being paid. You can't do another job [because of the contract], but they're not paying you!

I asked the company to release me, "pretty please, with sugar on top!" Everyone in SM said ok—except for Lee Su-man—he was furious. They'd kept him out of the loop [with her situation]. So we met, and he personally brought me back. Suddenly, my old manager got me on YTN [a TV station], and they moved me from singing to acting. They wanted to market me as something else. I was in a stage musical, and a sitcom. But then my manager did something wrong, and got fired. I was out again.

K-pop dances: Recently, they've been bringing in choreographers from overseas. They'll make a "point dance" [a dance based around a special concept, to help the group become more famous]. They'll give names to certain dances—*eongdeongi-chum* ("butt dance'), or Psy's horse dance, for example. The dance can come first, and then the song is made to match it.

Differences between big K-pop labels: Practice is pretty much the same, although at YG you have more say. SM is more of a pop factory, so you'll never see an indie or R&B style artist there. SM makes idols, JYP isn't quite so cookie-cutter—they like to have two percent imperfection. YG makes hip-hop and R&B, which is different. Nowadays, Cube Entertainment is coming up, with B2ST and G.Na. The CEO used to work for JYP, and he took a lot of their old trainees.

Plastic surgery: I have a bump in my nose, and they said, "You have to do something about that. Don't you want to look prettier?" But I didn't. Most of them do have plastic surgery, though. And botox or eyelid surgery isn't even considered plastic surgery any more. Botox here, filler there, it's nothing special. To say that there's any celebrity who has never done anything, it's a lie!

Image-making: You start off with a clean image, and then make it sexy when you do your comeback. When they hit a certain age, they start taking their clothes off.

The future of K-pop: We've done boy bands and girl groups, now let's try and see some actual talent. What's really sad in Korea is that talented people can't get air time, because of all these idol groups. I hope broadcasters will show more talented singers and target a broader appeal.

Above A public performance event held by D-Unit, a female vocal group that debuted in 2012. In any one year, labels will launch dozens of groups like this, in the hope that one or two might make it big. D-Unit have released two albums, but as of 2013, were still waiting for their first proper hit.

THE BEST KOREAN MUSIC YOU'VE NEVER HEARD

Frankly, I'm not a fan of K-pop. But that doesn't mean I don't love Korean music. The stuff I like is mostly made by indie musicians. Because the industry in Korea is so heavily dominated by manufactured girl and boy bands, it has long been difficult to turn on the TV and see bands who just formed for the love of music. So to find the "real deal" in Korea, you have to go and look for it. Here are my entirely subjective recommendations:

Third Line Butterfly My absolute favorite. They blend aggressive, grungy guitar meltdowns with sweet melodies and a healthy dollop of experimentalism. They aren't for everyone, although the *Hankyoreh* newspaper selected their most recent album *Dreamtalk* as their album of the year for 2012.

Asoto Union/Windy City Drummer/singer Kim Banjang's funk outfit Asoto Union folded in the mid 2000s, after releasing one brilliant album. Mr. Kim then went on to form Windy City, who still bring the funk, but also have a huge reggae influence. They have released several albums and EPs, and are known for their live performances. I saw them play a three-hour set once.

Rollercoaster These are the most "poppy" group on my list, and among the most musically talented. Their best album, *Sunsick*, blends Latin, jazz, pop, rock, and sounds almost too cool to have been made by humans. They are representative of the so-called "Fluxus Records Sound," along with Clazziquai Project, who are also worth checking out. Unfortunately, Rollercoaster have now gone their separate ways, with singer Cho Won-sun having released a solo album.

Byul.org (Moim-byul) Cho Tae-sang and friends have been running Byul.org as an artistic and musical collective for well over a decade. They produce a magazine, make video art installations, and release records; even Mr. Cho's day-job is an artistic one—he has his own architecture and design firm. They are also known for their love of drinking (I have experienced this first-hand). I would recommend starting with their songs "*Taepyeongyang*" ("Pacific") and "*Mongcheongideul*" ("Idiots").

Galaxy Express A mega-loud, leather-clad garage rock three-piece, Galaxy Express have toured the UK, the US, and East Asia. Their first album, *Noise on Fire*, is a masterpiece of no-nonsense rock n' roll.

Idiotape Two knob-twiddlers and one powerful drummer make Idiotape an extraordinary live act at festivals and clubs alike. Check out "Even Floor" and "Pluto" to see why. Bleeping noises have rarely sounded so exciting.

The Black Skirts The Black Skirts' leader, Korean-American Bryan Cho, is a master of pop hooks and singalong melodies. Debut album *201* is one of the best Korean albums of recent years.

Yamagata Tweakster I can't decide whether this guy is a performance artist, a musician, or a situationist joker. He shows up on public streets dressed in outlandish clothes, singing songs about rice farming, sexual topics, and Korean society. He uses a radio mic, enabling him to go up to strangers and dance with them. A true original who you absolutely ought to seek out on YouTube—and in concert if you get the chance.

Plastic People This band make wistful, acoustic songs backed up by bongo drums and melodica—though sometimes you'll hear a fuzzed-up rock guitar in the mix, too. Male/female harmonies add to the pleasure. Try their album *SNAP*, or songs like "*Woorideuleui Yeoreum*" ("Our Summer").

Delispice A modern rock band who have been around since their debut hit "*Chau Chau*" in the late 1990s, Delispice have gone on to release seven albums in total. They can be quite derivative of Britpop at times, but there is no doubt that a Delispice record will always contain a few gems.

An Interview with: Jaurim Vocalist, Kim Yoon-ah

Since the late 1990s, Jaurim have been one of Korea's best loved bands. Unusually for a group who formed without the direction of a record label, they have crossed over into the mainstream. Their singer, Kim Yoon-ah, is known for her emotionally powerful lyrics and strong stage presence. Her star quality is the main factor in Jaurim's success. Here, she gives her thoughts on her own music, and the state of the industry in Korea.

How did Jaurim get started?
From my middle school days, I enjoyed writing and singing my own songs. I went on to play in a few amateur bands when I was a university student, and as time went by I came to meet the future members of Jaurim, one by one.

Can you describe why you wanted to play music and join a band. What feeling does that give you?
Music has been a part of my life from a very early age. I was captivated by the fusion of melody and words, and the hidden emotion in melody. As I came to realize I had melodies and stories within me, I started to write my own songs.

A band is a very attractive "system" for a singer-songwriter. It completes the whole process of making music. With my fellow band members, I still feel joy even now in making music.

How would you describe Jaurim's musical style to newcomers?
We make music with a simultaneous pop and rock influence, with a theme of human nature and life. It may be mysterious or endlessly bright, beautiful or mischievous, but at the core our music is about human sadness, like the blues.

It seems as though every time I go to a noraebang, at least one person selects a Jaurim song. Why do you think this is?
Every time we make an album, we try to make a few songs that everyone at a concert can sing along to. So naturally, people might also like to sing them at the *noraebang*. I guess its because they make people feel good, right?

How does a band make the jump from Hongdae clubs to mainstream popularity?
If you look at the route Jaurim took from the indie clubs of Hongdae to the mainstream, I think it was all about the power of mass communication. Anyway, the biased, one-sided Korean music industry means that the market for indie music is small. Indie music doesn't enter the charts. Because of this, people don't know that there are so many great bands overflowing with creative energy. It's just a minority of people in Hongdae who go to live clubs and buy albums.

Above Korean B-boys practice some moves.

Jaurim If you like *noraebang*, you'll probably be familiar with their songs "Hey Hey Hey" or "Magic Carpet Ride."

How do people usually react when a young person in Korea says "I'm going to join a band"?

Many Koreans don't think of it as entirely positive, because of the issue of how you'll make a living out of music. But things are a lot better than they were compared to 1997, when we made our debut.

What is your opinion on the state of the music industry in Korea? Is it improving?

In this environment where music is sold extremely cheaply, only music distribution companies are able to grow. Digital music (i.e. mp3s) is sold at an abnormally low price, around one tenth of the international average. And the majority of what consumers pay goes to the distributor, rather than the musician or the record label.

If you're not an artist who is known well enough to get money from concerts and advertising, or if you can't scrabble together some other source of income, your future in music is pretty negative. If this situation doesn't change, the future of the whole of Korean music will be bleak.

However, in terms of musical content, when I look at younger artists pouring their hearts into their music, and when I

look at the new diverse promotional tools we can use, I still feel there's a future worth looking forward to.

I think it's really great that we have idol groups that are going abroad and have been doing well in the international scene for a number of years, singing songs in Korean. But its my hope that rather than just idol stars within the bounds of K-pop, we could have a diverse range of musicians playing songs in Korean on the international stage.

Is there too much manufactured music (i.e. boy bands, girl groups) in Korea?

Of course, I think there's a lot of it. But that isn't just true of Korea. Rather, it is the case that such groups appear more in the media here. Rather than such manufactured and trained groups, it would be good if naturally-formed bands and singer-songwriters would be able to use the power of mass communication to make people aware of their music.

If a rock music fan landed at Incheon Airport and asked you, "Where can I hear good music?" and "What bands should I listen to?" what would you say?

I recommend Sanullim, EoEoBu Band, Gukkasten, The Black Skirts, and of course, Jaurim! Look up the schedules for Hongdae live clubs and listen to a broad range of indie bands who are overflowing with energy!

THE LAND OF B-BOYS

Though you would never guess it, Korea is a break dance powerhouse. The dance form, which emerged in New York in the 1970s, has a short but illustrious history here. According to many sources, American soldiers first brought it to Korea during the 1980s, but it was not until 1997 that a native Korean B-boy culture began to take off.

Apparently, the spark was a video brought over by John Jay Chon, a Korean-American hip-hop enthusiast. He handed a VHS tape of a Los Angeles break dance contest over to the Expression Crew, a group of dancers he met in a club. They made copies of the tape, and distributed it to like-minded friends. Soon, its contents were serving to inspire an entire movement.

TOP KOREAN CREWS

Just five years later, the Expression Crew—directly influenced by John Jay Chon's video—ended up winning the most prestigious international B-boy contest, the Battle of the Year. And since then, Korean crews have dominated this competition, having won in 2004, 2005, 2007, 2009, and 2010. One crew, the Gamblerz, was for a time the world's most respected break-dance group. Today, the best team from Korea is the oddly-named Morning of Owl crew. Other leading outfits include the JinJo Crew, Project Soul, and the Extreme Crew.

The Extreme Crew have also been taking the form in new directions. They are noted for their musical, *The Ballerina who Loved a B-boy*, which

naturally features break-dance and ballet, but also popping and jazz dance. It is a non-verbal musical, meaning that it can be enjoyed by anyone regardless of language differences. Similarly, there have been attempts to blend break dance with martial arts such as Taekwondo. Backing music featuring hip-hop beats layered under traditional Korean instruments such as the *gayageum* has also become very common. B-boying in Korea has moved away from the street, and become a major form of mainstream entertainment.

WHY KOREA?

It is hard to say why Koreans fell so hard for B-boying. Perhaps it owes much to the efforts of Expression Crew, and the other early pioneers. In interviews, some members of that generation have said that break dance was a way of temporarily escaping the pressures of Korea's hyper-competitive society and tough educational system. Ironically, their international dominance may also partly be a result of that: when second best is never good enough, your life will be hard—but you'll be more likely to excel.

Right The Ballerina Who Loved a B-boy

Ballads and *Bbongjjak*

If you aren't one of the cool indie kids, and you don't like K-pop, what Korean music is there to listen to? There are two types of distinctively Korean types of popular music that have millions of loyal fans of all ages: "Ballad" and *Bbongjjak*.

What is a Ballad?

"Ballad" of course is not a Korean word, but it is used in Korea to denote a very specific kind of slow, emotional song. Their lyrics are invariably about lost love, or some other tragedy-laden theme. Ballad is a genre in itself, and vocalists go through specialized training to perfect the warbly, emotive voice that all ballad singers possess. The fact that Ballad is so popular is a reflection of the *han* culture of Korea, in which sadness is celebrated.

Music videos for Ballad songs lay the emotion on thick. Often, the central theme is the death of one of the characters. A stereotypical Ballad video might feature: a lover being hit by a car and lying in hospital, leaving the protagonist to cry and pray for the best; a man fighting a group of gangsters who had been harassing his girlfriend, and being killed in the process; or, the death of a beautiful woman from cancer or some other disease.

If this kind of catharsis sounds like your cup of tea, then try these singers out: Sung Si-kyung, Tim, MC The Max, Gummy, Fly To The Sky, Byul, and Kim Beom-soo.

Hongdae Korea's heartland of youth culture, music—and gigantic inflatable dolls, apparently!

The *Bbongjjak* Singalong

Frankly, Ballad isn't my cup of tea. But *Bbongjjak* kind of is. *Bbongjjak* (also known as "Trot") is shamelessly jolly music with a one-two oompah-oompah type rhythm, with what could be called a "Casio keyboard" style of instrumentation. It is a descendant of Japanese *enka* music, which heavily influenced Korea during the colonial era. *Bongjjak* was the most popular kind of music in the 1960s—cool kids listened to Western rock n' roll or jazz back then, but the masses loved *Bbongjjak* singers like Nam Jin and Lee Mi-ja.

Today, *Bbongjjak* is mostly enjoyed by old people. If you've ever been picked up by an older Korean taxi driver, chances are the music on his stereo will have been *Bbongjjak*. And if you've ever taken a trip into the Korean countryside, you will probably have seen big tour buses full of seniors blasting out the *Bbongjjak* and singing along as they go. (Such buses may also have *noraebang* machines, disco lights, and a plentiful supply of booze.)

Bbongjjak has undergone a slight renaissance in the past few years. There are a number of younger artists making their living in the genre. The most famous is Jang Yoon-jung, whose biggest hit was the delightfully camp *"Eomeona!"* (which roughly translates to "Oh My God!"). Then there is Park Hyun-bin, who had his first hit in 2006. Believe it or not, there is even a techno *bbongjjak* singer named Yi Bak-sa.

SINCHON AND HONGDAE

Back in the 1980s, the Sinchon district of Seoul was the heartland of Korean music culture. Live music clubs and bars playing vinyl records were all the rage. Some still exist—my own favorite is a tiny wood-panelled place called Damotori, which blasts out songs by classic Korean acoustic singer-songwriters like Kim Kwang-seok on a superannuated record player.

But rising rents ended up pushing many of the arty and broke down the road, to the area near Hongdae (Hongik University). Some time in the 1990s, Hongdae actually ended up eclipsing Sinchon. Bars devoted to different types of music, from reggae to metal, sprung up; then followed nightclubs, concert venues, theaters, and even Korea's largest concentration of lesbian bars. Roadside food stalls sell everything from *ddeokbokki* (rice cake in spicy sauce) to tacos and Japanese *takoyaki* balls.

HONGDAE: THE CAPITAL OF COOL

Today, Hongdae is a byword for alternative culture and artiness. "Gangnam Style" has a definite meaning, but so does "Hongdae Style." The stereotypical Hongdae person listens to music you've never heard of, watches independent cinema, and is a master of cheap living (having disdained mainstream consumerist culture). He or she still manages to look cool, though. Ironically, the hipness of Hongdae may end up being its downfall. Rents have become expensive, so any quirky establishment now struggles to survive. Ubiquitous chains like Lotte's Angel-in-us cafe have started taking their place. The really cool people are already moving on to Mullae-dong, just a few stops away on Seoul Metro line two. They are opening collective spaces for artists, and indie music venues such as the distinctly uncommercial Lowrise. The reason? Just like Hongdae once was, Mullae is dirt cheap.

WHERE TO HANG OUT IN HONGDAE
Hongdae is still pretty cool though, I must admit.
Here are a few places you should check out:

Noliteo This is a small park in which bands, DJs, sellers of arts and crafts, and drinkers gather. A great place to hang out on a Friday or Saturday night.

Reggae Chicken A bar that serves fried chicken and cold beer, and plays reggae music. There's nothing about that combination that I don't like. And just one floor above it is Sunshine, a great little music venue where I once did a spot of amateur DJ-ing.

Ding Dong Charming cafe with exactly one upstairs table, reachable only by ladder.

Samgeori Pocha A gigantic Korean-style bar that every young person in Seoul knows, serving standard fare such as clam soup and *soju*.

Soo Noraebang This is a "luxury" *noraebang*, with fancy decor and free ice cream for all customers. Possibly the most famous *noraebang* in all of Korea.

Vinyl Purveyors of cocktails that come in vinyl pouches. You can even buy drinks through the window, to take away; this is just as well, because the actual bar is so small that ten people would struggle to fit into it.

Bbang (acoustic); DGBD (punk) Evans (jazz); Strange Fruit (indie); Badabie (indie); Soundholic (mostly rock); Club FF (rock); and Sangsang Madang (a bit of everything). Try these concert venues to discover interesting new music.

Street art is reason enough to visit Hongdae. Instead of painting over it, some building owners encourage it, as it brings uniqueness to the area.

The green sign to the right is the metro stop for up-and-coming Mullae. Mullae could potentially be the Hongdae of ten years from now.

235
문 래
Mullae
文 來

A DJ plays at a "headphone party," in Noliteo, Hongdae.

Passers-by stopping for a quick cocktail from a plastic pouch bought through the window of Vinyl, the coolest little bar in Hongdae.

KOREAN MUSIC LEGENDS

K-pop acts come and go. But here are a handful of older musical legends who have stood the test of time:

Cho Yong-pil from Acrofan, 2013.

Shin Joong-hyun, whom I was lucky enough to interview a couple of years back.

Seo Tai-ji Nicknamed the "president of culture" by young people in the 1990s, Seo Tai-ji almost single-handedly brought hip-hop, electronic dance music, and heavy metal into the mainstream in Korea. He remains loved for songs like *"Gyoshil Idea"* ("Classroom Idea"), which criticizes Korea's harsh education system. These days he pops up once in a while with a sensational comeback record, before disappearing again. Existing beyond mere celebrity, Seo Tai-ji has unassailable cultural clout in Korea, in the way that John Lennon did in the West.

Shin Joong-hyun Mr. Shin is a guitar legend, a great songwriter, and also the nurturer of top vocal talents like Kim Chu-ja and Kim Jung-mi (both of whom are also well worth listening to). His heyday was the late 60s and early 70s, when he released songs like *"Mi-in"* ("Pretty Girl") and *"Areum-daun Gangsan"* ("Beautiful Rivers and Mountains"). Having refused to write a song praising dictator Park Chung-

hee, he became the target of police harassment and was eventually tortured and imprisoned for four years, after being caught in possession of marijuana. Thankfully, he is still active today, though well into his 70s. I saw him play a great show in December 2012.

Cho Yong-pil During the 1980s, Cho Yong-pil reigned supreme. He once drew an audience of over a million people in Busan, thanks to hits like *"Dolawayo Busan-hange"* ("Come Back to Busan Port") and *"Yeohaengeul Ddeonayo"* ("Leaving on Holiday"). You simply cannot live in Korea without knowing the latter song—28 years after its release, it is still played everywhere. The now sixty-something Mr. Cho also made a very well-received comeback in 2013, with the single "Hello."

Kim Kwang-seok The archetypal tragic troubadour, Kim Kwang-seok died by his own hand in 1996. He left behind a body of acoustic folk songs

beloved by millions of Koreans. One of them, *"Ideungbyeong Pyeonji"* ("Letter from a Private") concerns the story of a young soldier, and touches the hearts of those who are either conscripted, or have a loved one in the army—which means everyone.

Patti Kim No one beats Patti Kim for career longevity. She started singing rock n' roll for the US Army in 1959 (Cho Yong-pil and Shin Joong-hyun also learnt their trade this way) and went on to produce a string of pop hits from the 1960s onwards, such as *"Motijeo"* ("Can't Forget You"). She finally retired in 2012.

Kim Hyun-shik Despite dying of liver cirrhosis at the age of just 32, Kim Hyun-shik left behind six albums of well-loved folk and rock music. He also worked with legendary 1980s band Sinchon Blues. Knowing time was running out, he escaped from hospital in late 1990 to record his final album. He did not live to see it released.

Seo Tai-ji, a most enigmatic and popular Korean musician.

WANNABE A STAR?

Gaining entry into the world of K-pop takes years of vocal and dance training, and possibly a fair amount of plastic surgery. The Hongdae indie scene is very democratic, though—the only requirement is enthusiasm. If you can play an instrument, there will always be people who will want to meet you and jam. And if you're good, getting gigs won't be too difficult.

But where do you practice? When I was a teenager, we would jam in friends' garages. This is only an option for the richest Koreans, though. Most people live in apartments, so hammering away on a drum kit at home is out of the question. I live in a tiny type of apartment called an "officetel" (that being another example of Konglish), so I haven't even dared to plug my electric guitar in once.

BAND PRACTICE ROOMS

Korea has a *bang* (room) for everything. You can hire private rooms to watch DVDs, sing karaoke, and you can even hire meeting rooms in big cafes when you have something serious to discuss. So it stands to reason that there are also "band rooms." For around 20,000–30,000 won per hour, you and your bandmates can hire out a private, soundproofed room equipped with a drumkit, amplifiers, microphones, mixers, and a PA system. Long term rooms are also available—pay 500,000 won a month, and you can practice whenever you want.

A band practice room in the Hongdae area.

Hongdae naturally has the greatest concentration of band rooms, but you'll find them dotted all over Seoul and other big cities. Busan has a few good ones around the National University area; when I first lived in Korea, I would practice at a band room there named Roca Rola. When confident enough, my friends and I would take what we had down to Soul Trane, a music club. We weren't very good, but the audience was usually polite at least.

Bigger band rooms may even have their own recording studios, which can be rented for a surprisingly cheap price. I also joined a band in Seoul for a while, back in 2004; we used to practice around Gangnam station. One day we just decided to record our jam for fun; we left the tape rolling for two hours, and came out with a professionally recorded collection of half-baked songs for just 80,000 won.

Nakwon Sangga Music Arcade

Getting hold of instruments is easy, especially if you are in Seoul: in the downtown Jongro district, there is a dedicated building full of music shops, called Nakwon Sangga. Be prepared to haggle, though—from what I've seen, foreigners, women, and newbies will be quoted over the odds! If you don't like the sound of that, the best way to get a good deal is on secondhand websites—for English, use Craigslist, and in Korean, Junggo Nara. *Junggo* means "secondhand" in Korean.

Busker Busker

The biggest "proper" band in Korea right now is Busker Busker, a soft rock three-piece consisting of vocalist/guitarist Jang Beom-joon, bassist Kim Hyung-tae, and drummer Brad Moore—a Canadian national who first met Jang and Kim whilst working as their English teacher at Sangmyung University. They came to prominence with their participation in the Superstar K audition show, but refused to sign a long-term contract with organizer CJ E&M, who they felt wanted to control them. Going it alone, their popularity continued to hit new heights: in October 2013, eight songs in the Korean top ten were theirs! For a non-corporate group—or indeed, any group—their success is extraordinary.

Psy's "Gangnam Style": A Worldwide Sensation

If you asked a hundred people to name a famous South Korean, I'm sure at least ninety-eight would say Psy. So who is the man behind the song that drove everyone crazy in the summer of 2012? I had a quick chat with him to find out.

Did you expect "Gangnam Style" to make you a worldwide sensation?

Not at all. There's a K-pop wave going on overseas, but that's almost all about boy bands. I've been around for 12 years in Korea, and just expected to maintain my position in my country with this song.

"Gangnam Style" just happened on YouTube, so I don't want to over-predict [long-lasting] success. I read the replies on YouTube, most of them said it's funny, right? I'm not thinking I'm gonna be a star. I don't think like that yet. But if there's a possibility, then why not?

Your songs are catchy, and your videos are always fun. Where do you get your ideas?

I've been doing these things for 12 years. I released my first single in 2001, with the same nuance as "Gangnam Style." I became famous from that single. When I released this new song, I thought, "I want to go back to the start," going back to my early style.

Korea was kind of strict in those days, and my lyrics were too much, too fast for my country at the time. They were like, "what the ****?" pardon me. I did the same kind of dancing back then, too. When I read the comments of overseas viewers on YouTube, I could see that they were the same as how Koreans reacted when I brought out my first record.

The Dance The success of "Gangnam Style" owes as much to the "horse dance" as it does to the actual song. Its choreographer, Lee Ju-sun, received a car from Psy as a thank you.

You went to Berklee College of Music, didn't you?

Yeah, but I was a freshman for ten years! I was so fresh! I didn't graduate at all!

What Korean music would you recommend?

Of course, mine! About so-called K-pop, people think it's just girl/boy band music. But that idea of K-pop is too narrow. I want to say that there's all kinds of Korean singers; so many great musicians, writers, and artists. There are a lot of artists in this country, but to people overseas, if they think it's just boy/girl groups, then that's too narrow. We have rockers, hip-hop people, ballad singers, R&B singers, and so on. [Author's note: sadly, Psy didn't want to name specific artists, because he thought he may offend anyone he left out.]

What is Gangnam Style?

Gangnam is the Beverly Hills of Korea. In the song, I call a specific girl and specific boy "Gangnam style." But I added a twist. You can't find any "noble" or Beverly Hills stuff in the video. For twelve years, my preference has been to make a twist.

Is there anything you want to show to people outside Korea?

If there's a chance I can gain fame in other countries, then of course I want to introduce and express my country's culture. My favorite activity is performing in concert, I'm a showman. I always want to express my country's emotion. I always try to remind people that though we're wearing Western clothes and doing Western things, we shouldn't forget that we're Korean. So I want to express my country's culture.

What does Korea have to offer the world?

Koreans are dynamic. It's our personality—dynamic and passionate—sometimes we're too passionate. Think about the World Cup in 2002! That's the obvious passion of Korea. In music, we have singers, composers, and creators who are so passionate and dynamic. So when people from overseas see it, they think it's hot. But our weak point is, our population is too small.

Who is your musical idol?

I admire, respect, and adore Freddie Mercury, my hero and role model. When he died, it was 1991. I was a middle school student. I wanted to go to Wembley Stadium for the tribute concert. He was my only role model, the one who made me want to start in music. I'm not like Queen, but in manner and showmanship, I respected Freddie Mercury my whole life.

PART 9

MOVIES AND

TELEVISION

Don't know your *Daejanggeum* from your *Jumong*? In Asia at least, you'd be in a minority. Korean TV drama series are now wildly popular. For me, Korean cinema is where it's at—though I'm biased, I'd have to say that Korea is one of the world's cinematic hotspots.

A KOREAN TV PRIMER

If you visit a Korean home, the first thing you may notice as you enter the living room is a gigantic flat-screen TV. As with mobile phones and other gadgets, Koreans like to be ahead of the curve. This is also a very consumerist society, so even people who can't really afford it will happily plonk down US$1500 on the latest Samsung TV.

The average person is too busy to actually spend much time watching it, though. Kids study all day long, and their parents work all day long. Maybe the only time everyone sits in front of the tube is when the Korean national soccer team is playing, or stars like Kim Yu-na or Son Yeon-jae compete in the Olympics.

Left Gaming programs attract big audiences in Korea.

THE MAIN BROADCASTERS

There are three main broadcasting companies in Korea. These are KBS, SBS, and MBC. KBS is state-owned, and SBS is private. MBC is unusual in that it is majority-owned by a state organization (the Foundation for Broadcast Culture), but gets its money from advertising. Until 1961 it was a private company, but President Park Chung-hee confiscated it from its original owner after his 1961 military coup. Each of the three networks operates a range of drama, comedy, kids animation, and sports channels. KBS, for instance, has main channels named KBS 1 and 2, KBS Prime (for culture and drama), KBS N Sports, and KBS W (a new channel for women). KBS also runs KBS World, an English-language station distributed worldwide on cable and over the Internet.

Above Famous SBS series, Running Man. This show is popular throughout Asia.

Left Rhythmic gymnast Son Yeon-jae. Ms. Son is also probably the number one dream woman for young Korean men.

WHAT'S ON KOREAN TV?

Korean drama series are popular in many countries these days. They're popular in Korea too, of course, but TV here also has a strong American influence. Koreans love *Mideu*—a contraction of "*Miguk* Drama" (*Miguk* being the word for "America"). There are channels like OnStyle and OCN, which are full of Prison Break, CSI, Sex and the City, and so on. Reality TV is omnipresent, too. And perhaps unfortunately, Koreans are also familiar with shows like Cheaters and Jerry Springer.

Religious broadcasting takes up a lot of airspace. There are several Christian stations, launched by megachurch pastors. But there is also BBS, the Buddhist Broadcasting Service. At any time of day, you can tune in to watch monks offering their thoughts on life and spirituality.

Foreign visitors often comment on Korea's love of gaming channels. As noted in the previous chapter, there are three channels that show live computer game contests. And there is even Baduk TV, a channel devoted to the strategic board game of *Baduk* (known as "Go" in Japan and the West). Baduk is a beautiful game, both simple and infinitely complex—but I'm sure I'd have a hard time spending a whole evening watching other people play it.

Above A big screen TV is a prerequisite in just about any Korean living room.

FIVE KOREAN TV SHOWS TO KNOW

Now let's take a look at some of the most influential individual shows on Korean TV.

Pororo

Pororo (see picture, right) is a friendly computer-generated penguin, who lives in Porong Porong Forest with his friends Loopy, Crong, Harry, Eddy, and Poby. A friend of mine who has a young daughter tells me that the show is "like crack for pre-schoolers." *Pororo* is a true cultural phenomenon, and a cash cow for creators Iconix Entertainment. He even makes money for North Korea, with part of the animation being completed in the joint North-South Kaesong Industrial Complex.

Having been sold in countries as diverse as Sweden, Uruguay, and Indonesia, *Pororo*'s power extends far beyond Korea. His brand value has been estimated at around a billion dollars. Scarce wonder that adults nickname him "*Potongryeong*" or "*Poneunim*"— meaning "President Pororo," or "Pororo God" respectively.

PD Sucheop

PD Sucheop (Producer's Notebook) is an investigative documentary show with a particular ability to generate controversy. In 2008, the show alleged that American beef was a lot less safe than people thought, resulting in huge street protests that shook the government. They also broke the story about Korea's former scientific hero Hwang Woo-seok having faked his cloning experiments, and made an episode criticizing former President Lee Myung-bak's flagship "Four Rivers Restoration Project" in 2010.

Governments fear and hate *PD Sucheop*. Probably for that reason, there is a lot of interference in the show from above. I know one producer who used to work on *PD Sucheop*, but was moved suddenly to non-programming duties by senior MBC management. The show as a whole is not as powerful as it used to be. Not to worry, though: these days, *Geugeoti Algoshipda* (I Want To Know That), an investigative show made by SBS, is filling the gap.

Above Anti-US beef import protestors.

Below left One of the hottest TV shows in Korea—Korea's Got Talent.

Korea's Got Talent

Just like everyone else in the world, Koreans have fallen in love with the talent contest. Korea's Got Talent (modeled on Britain's Got Talent) is a particularly powerful spring-board for stardom. The show received worldwide attention due to contestant Choi Sung-bong becoming a viral hit on YouTube. Young Mr. Choi had been homeless, but his performance of "Amazing Grace" brought the house down and made him a sensation.

Rival shows to Korea's Got Talent include Superstar K, and *Naneun Gasuda* (I am a Singer). All are very popular.

Muhan Dojeon

Since 2005, *Muhan Dojeon* (Infinite Challenge) has been the leading "variety" show in a country that loves variety shows. Comedians like Park Myeong-soo and Noh Hong-cheol—best known internationally as the man grinding his pelvis in the "Gangnam Style" video—are given ridiculous challenges to complete, such as playing tennis against Maria Sharapova, or football against Thierry Henry. Around 15 percent of Koreans tune in to watch this every Saturday evening.

Muhan Dojeon has been selected by viewers as the most beloved show on Korean TV several times. Korean celebrities line up to be on it. And despite having long surpassed its three-hundredth episode, it is still going strong.

KBS News 9

KBS News 9 is the leading news show in Korea, ranking ahead of MBC Newsdesk and SBS 8 News in viewing figures. Its anchors become major stars, and can easily enter politics later if they wish. Becoming a KBS News anchor is therefore one of the most sought-after jobs in Korea. Presenter Min Kyung-wook jumped ship in 2014, and became President Park Geun-hye's spokesman.

KBS News isn't without controversy, though. The Lee Myung-bak government was constantly accused of manipulating the media, and viewing figures fell in 2009 after criticism that this state-owned broadcaster's main news show was too "nice" to the president.

GAG-CON: SLAPSTICK AND SATIRE

An episode of Gag Concert (or "Gag-Con" to fans) will consist of around ten segments, each filmed before a studio audience. Segments feature outlandish characters doing over-the-top, slapstick routines—I have to admit that frying pan-to-the-face type comedy still does work in Korea. But Gag Concert mixes this with satire of contemporary social issues.

BEING TOP-RATED IS TOUGH

In 2013, the show received a warning from the Korean Communications Standards Commission for using impolite language towards the President; and before that, politician Kang Yong-seok tried to sue the makers of Gag Concert for insulting the National Assembly. He had been offended by a skit implying that politicians just acted nice with ordinary people before elections, quickly forgetting them afterwards. This all tells you that although Korea is now a democracy, there is still a long way to go in making the powerful embrace the spirit of democracy. Gag Concert in fact provides a valuable service in showing the Korean people this basic truth.

Gag-Con producers regularly interview members of the public to find out what topics they would like to see lampooned, and then go for the jugular. If a segment fails to get laughs,

it is quickly dropped in favor of something else. Gag Concert has a large number of performers, so competition between them to make the top-rated segments is tough.

Among current performers, two of the most popular also happen to be an item. Kim Ki-ri starred in a segment named *Bulpyeonhan Jinsil* (Inconvenient Truth), and met Shin Bo-ra (of *Yonggamhan Nyeoseok-deul*, or Brave Boys) on set. The two are now one of Korea's hot celebrity couples.

Above Shin Bo-ra, one of the stars of Gag Concert and half of a celebrity couple with Kim Ki-ri.

Below Cast members of Gag Concert.

GAG-CONTroversy

There is another side to the success story, though. Gag-Con was criticized heavily in early 2014 for making apparently cruel jokes about people's appearances. One sketch involved a chubby girl finding herself unwelcome as a cheerleader. Furthermore, controversy also ensued in February 2014 when performers appeared "blacked-up" in another sketch.

WHY ARE KOREAN TV DRAMA SERIES SO POPULAR?

There are several reasons for the success of Korean drama. The first is a boring, technical one. Following the economic crisis of 1997, the government came to see creative industries as a future growth driver, and so started to pour money into TV, cinema, Internet start-ups, and so on. This allowed studios to raise their quality whilst still producing cheaply. But this was only the beginning.

Korean drama has now become part of a "Korean dream," especially for people from poorer Asian countries. Korean shows usually have more than their share of rich, glamorous characters. These characters, along with Korean pop stars, and Korean goods such as cosmetics, LG televisions, and Samsung phones, form an irresistible package.

From left to right Secret Garden, The Chaser, and Scent of a Woman.

And because of Korea's Confucian legacy, the importance of family is usually emphasized in Korean dramas. Marriage is one of the major themes. Often, this means a marriage between a wealthy man and a poor but beautiful girl, presenting a kind of Cinderella story to the audience. This is a universal type of plot that anyone can be a sucker for. Classic "love triangle" stories are common, too—not many viewers can resist these. (For a twist on that theme, see the romantic drama Secret Garden).

A "TEAR JERKER" CULTURE?

But the most important factor of all is, in my humble opinion, *han* culture. Korea's art reflects its culture, and so the emotionalism of Korea is deeply embedded into drama serials too. There is usually a heavy tear-jerking element in a drama storyline. For instance, the drama *Yeoeuineui Hyanggi* (Scent of a Woman) revolves around a young lady who has just months to live. The dying beautiful woman angle is a very common one in Korean dramas, as it is in Korean music videos.

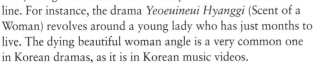

Male characters also exude a lot of emotion. Lead actors in particular combine masculinity—big fight scenes are common—and tenderness, entrancing the female viewer. Whether angry, sad, or in love, the male protagonist wears his heart on his sleeve. This is what makes Bae Yong-joon so popular with Japanese housewives.

AN EXCESS OF EMOTION?

For me, the emotionalism goes too far sometimes. I once started watching the 2012 series *Chujeokja* (The Chaser), the story of a policeman whose daughter is murdered by conspirators in a political plot. The bad guys in it are so bad, and the good guys so good, that I found myself wanting to jump into the screen and beat up the killers. Then I thought to myself, "I'm being completely manipulated here!" (especially since 2012 was a presidential election year). The melodrama was just too much, frankly—but I have to admit, The Chaser was a very successful show in Korea.

Menboong Breakdown

The show Gag Concert is also known for helping to popularize a large number of slang words and phrases. *Menboong*, for instance. This is a contraction of the English word "mental" and the Korean word *boongwai*, which means "breakdown" or "destruction." A whole segment of Gag Concert was called "*Menboong* School," leading *menboong* to become such an over-used word in 2012 that by October that year even hearing it caused me to suffer *menboong*.

Since the show airs on Sundays, viewers are able to start the new work or school week with a new Gag-Con phrase on their lips. On Monday lunchtime, it is normal to hear people using them, says Lee Chang-sup of the *Korea Times* newspaper: "Older managers and executives who miss the show are sure to be out of tune with their young subordinates," he adds. I remember myself seeing a well-known North Korea scholar, Professor Moon Chung-in, making a group of young conference attendees laugh by throwing in a quick *menboong*. With just one word, he had made himself cool in their eyes. That is the power of Gag Concert.

THE WINTER SONATA CRAZE

Probably the first bona fide overseas hit was Winter Sonata, a love story starring Bae Yong-joon and Choi Ji-woo. First broadcast in 2002, Winter Sonata became huge in Japan, and made a star out of Bae Yong-joon, who is now universally known by Japanese fans as *Yonsama*. His arrival at Narita Airport once caused a fan riot.

Even more successful was *Daejanggeum*, a 2003 period drama starring Lee Young-ae. It became the most successful ever drama show in Hong Kong, topped the ratings polls in Iran, and appeared on screens in countries as diverse as Zimbabwe, Australia, Hungary, and Venezuela.

Today, there are tourists who come from China and Japan just to look at the sites where Winter Sonata, *Daejanggeum*, and other dramas were filmed. This is why Winter Sonata, for instance, has generated US$2.7 billion for the Korean economy since its release.

Korean dramas have done well in the unlikeliest of places. A friend of mine who is married to the star of a historical drama told me once, "The president of Iraq and his wife love my husband's show, so they invited us to their palace. And then whenever we went out in public, he was mobbed."

Right Namiseom (Nami Island), the picturesque location that featured in Winter Sonata and has now become a major tourist attraction.

Winter Sonata was also made into anime.

A BLUFFER'S GUIDE TO KOREAN TV DRAMAS

Let's now leave Winter Sonata and *Daejanggeum* behind and take a look at a few other popular drama series:

Iris This stars Lee Byung-hun and Kim Tae-hee, one of Korea's leading *eoljjang* actresses. The story is a little unusual in that it revolves around an international spy conspiracy, rather than anything romantic. But that definitely isn't a bad thing. Iris had a budget of almost US$20 million, making it the most expensive Korean drama ever.

High Kick This one earns praise from fans due to its social commentary and portrayal of Korean family life. High Kick features multiple plot lines and an ensemble cast. It spawned two sequel series as well.

Eungdaphara **1997 (Reply 1997)** This drama switches back and forth from the present day to 1997, when the main character was a "fan girl," obsessed with real-life boy band HOT. Viewers loved the show's warmth and humor. The popularity of Reply 1997 also reflects the growing trend for nostalgia among younger Korean adults.

Also look out for its sequel, *Eungdaphara* **1994 (Reply 1994)**, which found huge popularity in the winter of 2013–14 in Korea. Many fans judged it to be even better—and richer in nostalgia—than the original.

Coffee Prince This is the implausible story of a woman who pretends to be a man in order to get a job at a coffee shop that only hires handsome guys. She then falls in love with the owner, who encourages her to become a barista. Stars popular "Korean Wave" celebrities Yoon Eun-hye and Gong Yoo.

Chuno **(The Slave Hunter)** Lead actor Jang Hyuk received an International Emmy nomination for his portrayal of a Joseon Dynasty man driven by the desire for revenge. Where most dramas are over the top, this one is smartly-written, well-acted, and beautifully presented.

Full House Another implausible but charming romance, about a woman who is swindled out of her house and has to enter into a marriage of convenience with a famous actor in order to get it back.

Kkotboda Namja **(Boys Over Flowers)** A cutesy high school drama about a poor girl accepted into an elite school on a scholarship, who then goes on to charm the snooty boys. Boys Over Flowers was a huge success around Asia.

Shinsaeui Pumgyeok **(A Gentleman's Dignity)** In one of the big hits of 2012, "Korean Wave" idol Jang Dong-gun plays a forty-something playboy who ends up falling for a school teacher. It is also a tale of friendship, centered around Jang and three other men, who have known each other since their school days.

Jumong This is the story of the founder of Goguryeo, one of the "three kingdoms" that existed before Korea was united. The show ran for 81 episodes, and gained viewership ratings of over 80 percent in Iran. Its star, Song Il-guk, has an interesting background: his mother was an actress and parlimentarian; his grandfather a legendary gangster; and, his great-grandfather an even more legendary Korean independence fighter.

KOREAN CINEMA: THE GOLDEN ERA

The first Korean movie I saw was an off-the-wall sex comedy named *Saekjeuksigong* (Sex is Zero), starring Ha Ji-won and Lim Chang-jeong. The first half was like *American Pie* times ten, but as the story progressed, extreme seriousness took over and themes like attempted suicide came into play. It was a rather strange introduction to Korean cinema.

TWO GREAT ACTORS

But I was lucky to have arrived in Seoul in 2004. Back then, Korean cinema was enjoying a golden period of creativity, one that lasted from roughly 1998 to 2005. So I moved on from *Saekjeuksigong* to *Salineui Chueok* (Memories of Murder), a stunning serial killer mystery considered one of the best Korean movies of all time. Its star, Song Kang-ho, was one of the heroes of the era: he excelled as a North Korean soldier in *JSA*; a spy in *Shiri*; and as a salaryman-turned-wrestler in the hilarious *Banchik-wang* (The Foul King).

His main competitor for the heavyweight acting crown was Choi Min-sik, whose turn in *Old Boy* as a mysteriously imprisoned man was a triumph of imagination. *Old Boy* made Mr. Choi's name outside Korea, but there were other classics: *Failan*, my favorite Korean movie of all time, in which he plays a a low-life gangster; and *Chihwaseon*, in which he plays a troubled artist from the late Joseon era.

THE BURSTING OF THE BUBBLE

Sadly, those days could not last. Because of the impressive work done in the golden period, combined with the growing success of Korean movies abroad, studios became complacent. Quality suffered, and eventually, commercial success disappeared, too.

Movies starring famously beautiful actress Jun Ji-hyun illustrate this point: her defining role was in *Yeopgijeogin Geunyeo* (My Sassy Girl) back in 2000; audiences loved her performance so much that Ms. Jun became the go-to star to hire when you needed a hit but lacked a storyline. Subsequent Jun Ji-hyun movies, like *Yeochinso* (Windstruck) and *Daisy* failed to live up to critical or commercial expectations. Her personal star remains undiminished, though.

Jang Dong-gun, an actor best known for his leading roles in the movies *Friend* and *Taegukgi*.

Korea's Top-Earning Actors

Unsurprisingly, Winter Sonata star Bae Yong-joon commands the highest appearance fees in Korean TV drama. He can demand around US$200,000 per episode. His nearest rival, Kwon Sang-woo, received $100,000 per episode for appearing in Bad Love. Other well-paid stars include Kim Tae-hee and Song Seung-hun, who each were paid $90,000 per episode of My Princess, and Lee Byung-hun, who took home just slightly less for his role in Iris.

Jang Dong-gun has long been a mainstay of Korea's top earning celebrity charts. But he's also a member of *yeongi-pa*—the group of big stars who are also considered to have superior acting ability (the usual criticism is that good-looking stars can't act their way out of a paper bag). Jang was chosen by a panel of drama professors as the best among Korea's big-name actors in 2011.

Here are a few more masterpieces from 1998–2005:

Bakha Satang (Peppermint Candy) A beautiful and tragic movie that captures the harsher realities of modern South Korean history, through the story of one man's life. Directed by Lee Chang-dong, a true artist and one who seems incapable of making bad movies.

Geuttaegeu Saramdeul (The President's Last Bang) A controversial movie by maverick director Hong Sang-soo, which presents the last moments of assassinated President Park Chung-hee. Its portrayal of President Park as a Japanophile enraged Korean conservatives. However, it is hard to deny that it is a very watchable and suspenseful movie.

Wangeui Namja (The King and The Clown) The most popular Korean movie ever at the time, this was the story of an itinerant (male) performer who captures the romantic attentions of King Yeonsangun, one of the most notorious rulers of the Joseon Dynasty. Homosexuality as an overt theme was new territory for a big-budget Korean movie, but mainstream audiences loved it.

Oasis Another Lee Chang-dong picture. This one depicts an unusual love story between a mentally challenged man and a woman afflicted by cerebral palsy.

From top left, clockwise: Save the Green Planet; actor Won Bin; The President's Last Bang; Peppermint Candy; The King and The Clown; Oasis

Taegukgi A huge, emotional epic that takes in the tale of two brothers separated by the Korean War. Starring Won Bin.

Chingu (Friend) A brilliant, bloody gangster epic set in Busan. It had a great impact on young Koreans, popularizing a whole range of Busan dialect swearwords. I even heard that kids in Pyongyang now use them, with some having seen the movie on smuggled USB sticks.

Jigureul Jikyeora (Save the Green Planet) This is a black comedy sci-fi horror thriller (yes, really) that defies accurate description. But watch it anyway.

The Best of a Bygone Era

Korean movie-making in the black-and-white era was heavily affected by politics. Following liberation from Japanese occupation in 1945, the authorities continued to censor movies as the Japanese had done; then, in 1950 came the war, which practically destroyed the movie industry in the way it did everything else. The late 1950s saw a commercial revival, in which director Shin Sang-ok and his actress wife Choi Eun-hee were the leading lights. The two are most famous in the west for being kidnapped in 1978 on the orders of cinema-obsessed Kim Jong-il, and brought to North Korea to make movies for him. However, their most renowned movie was made in South Korea in 1958—*Jiokhwa* (Flower of Hell) is the harsh tale of a man who steals from US military bases, and his girlfriend, who sells sex to its soldiers.

Poster for *Arirang*, a 1926 silent movie concerned with Korea during the Japanese occupation.

"COMMERCIAL FEATURES": THE LIFEBLOOD OF A KOREAN CELEBRITY

How does a Korean television personality get rich? Their biggest paydays don't come courtesy of KBS or MBC. The lion's share of their earnings comes from advertising. The same is true for pop stars, movie actors, and just about any other famous person. Whereas indiscriminately taking the *chaebol* dollar would be considered "selling out" in many countries, smiling in front of a washing machine or seductively drinking a bottle of green tea is a star's lifeblood in Korea.

Korea has a huge number of celebrities and semi-celebrities, and the existence of problems like illegal downloading of movies and music combined with this means that very few could survive without money from "CF" (a Konglish acronym for "Commercial Feature").

A BEEF WITH HYO-RI

Actress, model, and singer Lee Hyo-ri has been one of the country's top stars for over a decade, and is considered a sure bet to sell just about any product. So when the Korean beef marketing board paid her just over $300,000 to hawk their prime cuts, they thought they were on to a winner.

Unfortunately for them though, Ms. Lee announced herself as a vegetarian not long after. They ended up suing her to get the money back.

There are even stars who are criticized for only doing adverts. Actress Lee Young-ae hasn't made a TV show or appeared in a movie since 2005, but can still be seen selling products. Others do so many adverts that the companies hiring them become irritated at having to "share" their stars. Actor Jo In-sung and actress Kim Tae-hee promote a wide range of companies; and at the time of writing, the pretty-boy face of celebrity Song Jun-ki can be seen on adverts for products as incongruous as hamburgers, water coolers, and cosmetics.

Below Actor Jo In-sung promotes a wide range of products for various companies. Left Lee Young-ae. Top Kim Tae-hee is one of the most popular and in-demand product endorsers in Korea. She is best known for her roles in Korean dramas such as Iris, Love Story in Harvard, and My Princess.

The Man Who Says "No"

Popular indie crossover singer Jang Ki-ha is known for refusing to do adverts, and has spoken publicly about his desire to be known as a musician rather than a company promoter. But his is a rare case. A friend of mine who is slightly famous once told me, "I was offered 10 million won for doing a quick advert to sell some health drinks I'd never heard of. But it was easy money, so how could I say no?" To be honest, I think I'd find it hard to say no as well.

The High Rollers

"CF" do pay off very well for the top names: in 2011, 68 Korean stars were able to charge US$500,000 or more for one advertising campaign. Furthermore, 57 percent of Korean advertising features celebrities, a figure much higher than most other countries. World champion figure skater Kim Yu-na (referred to as "Yu-na Kim" in the foreign media) is an inescapable fixture on Korean TV, as a spokesmodel for an extraordinary range of products. She is one of a small number of famous people who can be referred without her family name (like Madonna), and is the number one celebrity in terms of "likeability" according to the Korea CM marketing institute. This means she can attract big bucks from Samsung, LG, KB Financial Group, Maeil Dairy, Maxim instant coffee, and even Hite beer. Though it seems strange to think of a figure skater advertising beer, consumers are happy to play along, such is Kim Yu-na's reputation. She earns an average of 1.2 billion won (about US$1.1 million) from each of her advertising campaigns.

In terms of overall earnings, pop group Girls' Generation make the most money from advertising—though they have to split their take nine ways. But on an individual basis, Psy is King. Since "Gangnam Style" made him the world's most famous Korean, he has raked in the money by advertising *soju*, mobile phone subscriptions, and *budae jjigae* stew. He even has his own moisturiser range. His earnings in 2012 alone were around US$28 million.

Olympic Gold medallist Kim Yu-na is the most beloved person in Korea, and companies will pay handsomely to trade on that status.

Kim Yu-na

Kim Yu-na hails from the city of Bucheon, close to Seoul. She began skating at the age of five, and won her first international competition at the age of just eleven. Being too young to compete in the 2006 Olympics, she entered the World Junior Championships, and won by some distance over Japanese rival Mao Asada.

Since coming of age, she has claimed world record scores in free skating and the short program, as well as Olympic Gold in 2010 in Vancouver.

Above Every main TV network showed 2010's gold medal moment on a loop. Even her practice sessions are treated as news.

Right Kim Yu-na (right) with her childhood hero, skating legend Michelle Kwan.

Opening ceremony of Busan International Film Festival

KIM KI-DUK

While the big studios are not managing to live up to the standards they set in the late 1990s and early 2000s, there are legions of talented independent directors and actors producing truly impressive works. The most famous of these is now Kim Ki-duk, a director revered in Europe for movies like *Spring, Summer, Autumn, Winter... and Spring* and *Samaria*. He won the Golden Lion prize at the 2012 Venice Film Festival for *Pieta*, the tough story of a relationship between a loan shark and a middle-aged woman. Mr. Kim is famed for working quickly, and with extremely small budgets. *Pieta* took twelve days to make, and had a budget of less than US$100,000.

Kim Ki-duk was a perennial outsider. His movies are notoriously violent, and have a bleak outlook drawn from his tough upbringing. The mainstream disdained him—so much so that he made a documentary in 2011 that centered mostly on how much he hated the movie industry and everyone in it. However, Korea loves anyone who puts the country on the map, and since his Venice win in 2012, he has become something of a hero.

THE ART OF CINEMA IN KOREA

For decades, Korea has been a cinema-obsessed country. But during the period of military dictatorship (1961–1987), directors were forced to comply with strict censorship regulations. Under Park Chung-hee, only "wholesome" stories were allowed. The general who followed him, Chun Doo-hwan, had a slightly different approach: he pursued the so-called "3S policy" (Sports, Screen, and Sex). He wanted to give mindless entertainment to the masses, to take their minds off more serious things. He therefore relaxed regulations on screen nudity, for instance, but still ruthlessly cracked down on anything that criticized Korean society or the government.

This meant that when democracy finally arrived, a great amount of pent-up creativity was unleashed on the nation's screens. This wave of success inspired a generation of young people to enter film school. And even now, Korea has the world's highest per capita rate of film school enrolment.

THE EARLY 1960s

Between the removal of one dictator (Syngman Rhee) in 1960 and the arrival of a new one (Park Chung-hee) in 1961, a chaotic democracy filled the gap. Movie makers enjoyed unprecedented, but temporary, freedom. It is surely no coincidence, then, that two of the greatest ever Korean movies came to be made in this short period.

The first is *Hanyeo* (The Housemaid). This is a tense psychological thriller about an unhinged housemaid who seeks to exact revenge upon her employers. It also operates on another level as a critique of contemporary Korean society. The "housemaid" of the title was apparently so convincing that audiences would scream out at her with rage.

The second is *Obaltan* (Stray Bullet). *Obaltan* is not a feel-good movie by any means, as it unflinchingly portrays the poor, miserable lives of a man and his family as they struggle to cope with poverty and mental illness. But it is a product of its era—and an extraordinary one at that.

Both of these movies are available at the Korean Film Archive's YouTube channel, with English subtitles. Here are three other old classics you can see there:

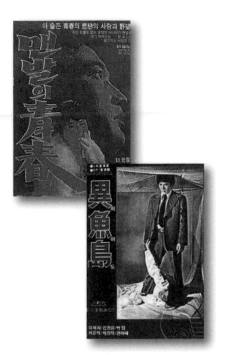

***Menbaleui Cheongchun* (Barefooted Youth)** This is the career-defining movie of Shin Seong-il, the tough guy leading man of the 1960s. A bad-boy meets a diplomat's daughter, and her parents' opposition to their union leads them to commit suicide. See also *Cho-woo* (Early Rain) for a similar turn from Shin Seong-il.

Iodo A young man leaves his remote island home and disappears, leaving a businessman suspected of killing him to come and investigate for himself. The story is told through flashbacks, making it a complex movie to follow—but the payoff at the end is worth it.

Chilsu and Mansu Now-legendary actor Ahn Sung-ki plays one of the main protagonists in this tale of angry youth lashing out at authority.

RECENT INDIE MASTERPIECES

A major recent success is director O Muel, who released the harrowing *Jiseul* to critical acclaim in 2012. His depiction of Jeju island villagers hiding from mainland soldiers seeking to massacre them in the name of "anti-communism" in 1948—a true story—took the World Cinema Dramatic Grand Jury Prize at the prestigious Sundance Festival. Not bad for a movie costing just US$190,000 to make.

My own favorite of Korea's recent independent movies is *Ddongpari* (Breathless), made by young auteur Yang Ik-jun. I interviewed him once, and was sad to see that he was not really enjoying the movie's unexpected success. He clearly felt under pressure to produce more of the same. But it is hardly surprising. *Ddongpari* is a special movie, which deservedly won over a dozen awards at international festivals. Mr. Yang himself plays the main character, a street thug who develops a

friendship with a troubled high school girl. His co-star, Kim Kkobbi, is now a doyen of Korean indie cinema as well, thanks to that role.

ALSO WATCH

***Weonak Sori* (Old Partner)** Believe it or not, this is a super low-budget documentary about a farmer and his trusty cow. Sounds boring, right? Well, three million people went to the cinema to watch it, so it can't be that bad.

Romance Joe A movie-maker is sent to away to the countryside to finish a script. There, he meets a good-time girl who tells him a succession of fascinating tales. The movie thus becomes a series of stories within a story.

***Natsul* (Daytime Drinking)** Noh Young-seok made this movie with 10 million won. Sometimes, it shows. But this story of a put-upon youth who ends up going on an unexpected drunken odyssey in a small town is a winner, for its clever script and sense of humor.

A classic Chun Doo-hwan era movie poster. The 1980s dictator dramatically loosened restrictions on sexual content, as part of his 3S policy.

PART 10
VISITING
KOREA

When I wrote my previous book, *Korea: The Impossible Country*, I said to myself that the best compliment I could receive would be for someone to tell me, "I decided to visit Korea because of your book." But then I thought, that would be pretty unfair unless I could give them a few recommendations for cool places to visit in return...

GANGNAM—THE TRENDY SOUTHERN PART OF SEOUL

"If you have a son, send him to Seoul," went an old expression. The nation's capital city is a magnet for people, resources, and plenty more besides. Half of the population lives in or around Seoul. So, it wouldn't seem right to start by talking about anywhere else.

Seoul doesn't feel like one city, though. It feels like two: Gangnam (south of the river) and Gangbuk (north of the river). The former was built in the past forty years, whereas the latter has existed for centuries. The buildings look different, and the people are different, too—hence "Gangnam Style," which as everyone knows, refers to all that is flashy and nouveau riche.

But how does one experience Gangnam Style? Here are my suggestions:

Apgujeong Get out of the train at Apgujeong Rodeo station. Immediately you will see Galleria Department Store. Galleria is ground zero for designer labels and conspicuous consumption. And if you walk up the hill towards Cheongdam, you'll see gigantic Prada and Ferragamo shops, to name but a couple. Koreans spend five percent of their income on luxury goods, and a good chunk of that is spent on this one street.

Galleria Department Store: I can just about afford a cup of coffee here.

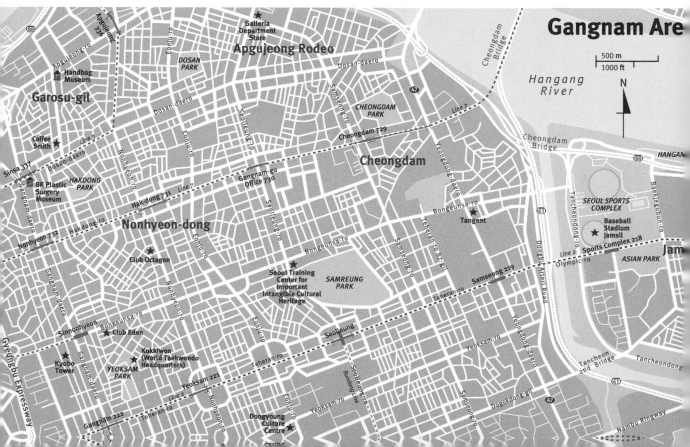

Garosu-gil (Sinsa station area)

Garosu-gil means "tree-lined street." But these days, Garosu-gil is known for its boutiques and restaurants. Coffee shops like Coffee Smith have long, open patios, designed for seeing and being seen. Fashionistas strut around in the hope that some blogger or photo-journalist will take their picture. And increasingly, tourists abound. The idea of Garosu-gil is summed up perfectly by the presence of the Simone Handbag Museum, a monument to Gangnam Style. For an even stranger—but no less Gangnam—museum, check out the BK Plastic Surgery Museum at the BK building. BK is such a successful plastic surgery clinic that it occupies an entire 16-story building.

Party Hard: The Nonhyeon-dong area

This district is a little rougher and readier than regular Gangnam. Enjoy *soju* at one of the many bars in the area, and then move on to one of Gangnam's "superclubs"—Octagon, or Eden. Both these clubs are the kind of places where people pull up outside in Ferraris, and are allowed to jump the queue because they're buying endless bottles of expensive vodka in the VIP area. And if you still have the energy, move on later to an "afterclub," such as Club 88, where the action continues until lunchtime the next day.

Baseball in Jamsil Jamsil Olympic Stadium is now home to the LG Twins, one of Korea's most successful baseball teams. Being British, I've no idea how baseball works. But the game is almost secondary—cheerleaders and mascots hype up the crowd, and beer is very much available to finish the job. A baseball game in Korea is a proper night out.

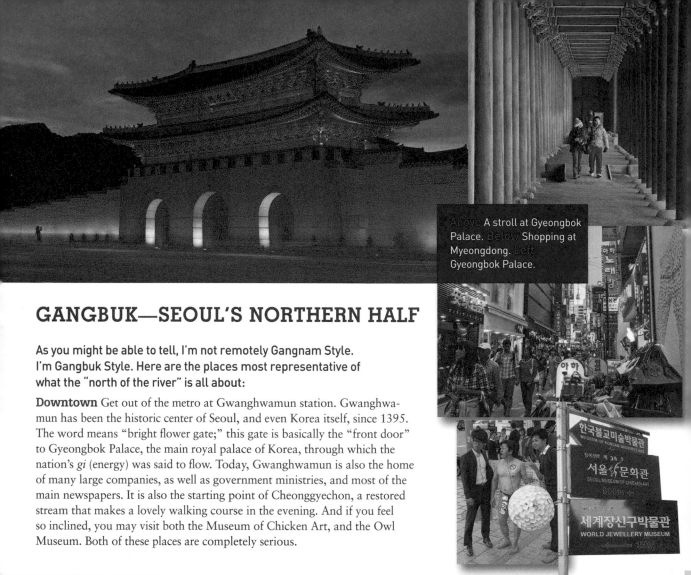

Above A stroll at Gyeongbok Palace. Below Shopping at Myeongdong. Left Gyeongbok Palace.

GANGBUK—SEOUL'S NORTHERN HALF

As you might be able to tell, I'm not remotely Gangnam Style. I'm Gangbuk Style. Here are the places most representative of what the "north of the river" is all about:

Downtown Get out of the metro at Gwanghwamun station. Gwanghwamun has been the historic center of Seoul, and even Korea itself, since 1395. The word means "bright flower gate;" this gate is basically the "front door" to Gyeongbok Palace, the main royal palace of Korea, through which the nation's *gi* (energy) was said to flow. Today, Gwanghwamun is also the home of many large companies, as well as government ministries, and most of the main newspapers. It is also the starting point of Cheonggyechon, a restored stream that makes a lovely walking course in the evening. And if you feel so inclined, you may visit both the Museum of Chicken Art, and the Owl Museum. Both of these places are completely serious.

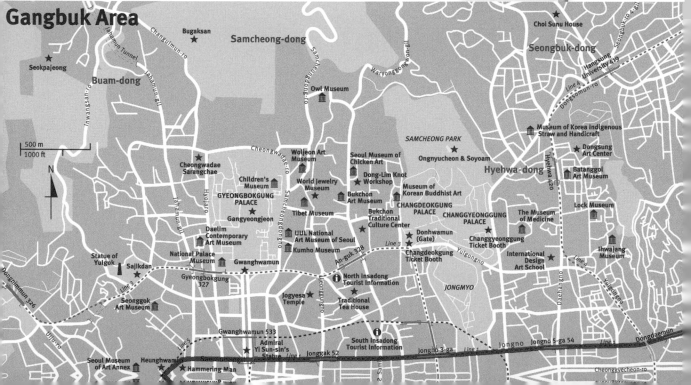

For a mad shopping experience, make the short walk to **Myeongdong**. I call it "mad" because I don't think I have ever seen a place so crowded in all my life. Myeongdong is where stereotypical Asian city scenes become reality—copious amounts of neon, weird and wonderful fashions, salespeople yelling at you as you go by—seemingly millions of people are packed into an area of a few square blocks. Myeongdong also has the ninth most expensive commercial real estate in the world.

For an almost-as-mad shopping experience, go to **Dongdaemun** in the evening. Buildings like Doota teem with individual stalls, each selling their own funky fashions until the early hours. Dongdaemun is also home to a large immigrant population, so if you ever wanted to try Uzbek or Nepali food in Korea, this is the place to go. Then check out the street market around nearby Dongmyo station, where old gentlemen sell the oddest items—I've seen portraits of all Korea's military dictators there, as well as quad bikes and antique typewriters.

Itaewon and Gyungridan Historically the "foreigner area" (in the way that Roppongi is to Tokyo), Itaewon is home to some of the best international restaurants in the city. Like Roppongi, it is also no longer as much of a sleaze-fest as it used to be—the "girly bars" targeting American servicemen are giving way to fancy wine bars, and the fake brand stalls seem to be on their way out, too.

Down the road is Gyungridan, where old-school Korean restaurants are found next to cocktail bars and little foreign-owned Greek, Italian, and Mexican restaurants. It is also home to the first branch of The Booth, a bar part-owned by yours truly!

Top Samsung Art Museum in Itaewon. **Left** Food stalls at Dongdaemun.

The Leafy North Just northeast of Gwanghwamun is Samcheongdong, a pretty, tree-lined district popular with dating couples. Keep going, and you'll reach Samcheong Park, where local workers go when they need to escape from the concrete jungle for an hour or so.

Also try Hyehwa-dong, Seoul's independent theater district, and home to a Philippine street market every Sunday afternoon. Then walk through the grounds of the nearby Sungkyunkwan University, and out of the back gate. That will set you on the trail for one of Seoul's best walks, over the mountain of Bugaksan. It's a trek that should take you a couple of hours, and provide you with some breathtaking views of the city. It also provides views of the presidential mansion—so photography is restricted. The route was also taken by North Korean commandos seeking to assassinate President Park Chung-hee in 1968. They were involved in a shoot-out with local officers, and as evidence, you can still see a bullet hole in one of the trees on Bugaksan.

On the way down from Bugaksan, you'll come out at a neighborhood called Buam-dong. Buam-dong is a relaxed but trendy enclave of funky coffee shops and restaurants. Also, take a look around Seongbuk-dong. Seongbuk-dong is where "the other half" live—beautiful houses nestle among beautiful scenery.

BUSAN: KOREA'S SECOND CITY

Because of my work, I have no choice but to live in Seoul. But if I did have a choice, I'd move to Busan in a heartbeat. It is a city of over three million people, but the presence of sandy beaches and sea air make Busan an infinitely more relaxed proposition. The food is pretty good, too. You can reach Busan from Seoul in three hours, on the 186 mph (300km/h) KTX train. Here's where to go when you get there:

Haeundae Beach A beach resort in the big city. Haeundae is home to five star hotels and love motels; live squid and American steak-houses; peaceful trekking routes and nightclubs; and, an aquarium. In the summer months, it is the number one fun destination in Korea. It's also home to Dalmaji Hill, a haven of cool coffee shops with great ocean views. Walk a little further along the coast, and you'll find Songjeong Beach—which is like another Haeundae Beach, only no-where near as developed. Apparently the surfing is quite good there, too.

Gijang If you head east from Songjeong Beach, you'll reach Gijang. Gijang has some great walks with ocean views, and extremely fresh seafood. Also, make sure to visit Yonggungsa, a Buddhist temple built into the rocky coastline.

Jagalchi Market This is a seriously large fish market, with architecture seemingly inspired by Sydney Opera House. Watch with morbid fascination as an *ajumma* lines up a live fish and slices its head clean off, before gutting the body, and cutting up the flesh into pieces. You can start eating it before the head has given up its last.

Then when you're done, go to nearby Taejongdae. Taejongdae is a beautiful country park overlooking the sea. It may well be one of the most attractive places in all of Korea.

Pusan National University Area Don't be confused by the fact that the university is "Pusan" whilst the city is "Busan." They are just different ways to

Busan is a working port city and center of fishing. But it is also home to some very futuristic-looking buildings, as well as the world's largest department store.

represent the same name in the Roman alphabet. Regardless, the area around Pusan National University is full of interesting bars and live music clubs. I used to favor Moo Monk, Soul Trane, and Interplay. I even sang a few times in the latter two. Another great music club is Vinyl Underground, located in the Pukyeong/Kyungsung University district.

Seomyeon This is the "downtown" of Busan, and in fact, it's a little bit like Myeongdong—lots of neon, too many people, and tons of shopping to be done. Seomyeon is particularly popular with Japanese tourists—also like Myeongdong!

JEJU ISLAND: THE "HAWAII OF KOREA"

Korean tourist brochures call Jeju the "Hawaii of Korea." That might be overdoing it a little—but Jeju does indeed have palm trees, sandy beaches, waterfalls, and a large volcanic mountain (Hallasan) at its center. The island also has a very strong tradition of shamanism, and some of the toughest old women you've ever seen—so-called *haenyeo* (sea women) dive 65 feet (20 m) under the sea, and hold their breath for several minutes while searching for abalone.

Gimnyeong Maze Park

If you visit Jeju, make sure you get lost in Gimnyeong Maze Park. The maze itself is fun, but its owner is the real star. Frederic Dustin is an American who has witnessed the complete transformation of Korea, having lived here for over fifty years. In his early days in Korea he worked in gold mining, being entrusted to carry the precious yellow stuff in his pockets all the way to Seoul. He is also partially credited with the introduction of basketball to Korea.

The famed *haenyeo* of Jeju, one of the great symbols of Korea.

THE WONDERS OF JEJU

Jeju also has Olle-gil, a 260 mile (422 km) walking trail that takes you all along the coast. The trail is broken into 21 sections, so you could do about one per day, stay in a different guesthouse each night, and complete the whole course in around a month if you had the time.

There are a great number of beaches; the most well-known is probably Jungmun, on the south side of the island. Jungmun is not far from Cheonjeyeon Waterfall, one of the most striking features on Jeju. The area also has lots of *minbak*—traditional guesthouses where you can rent a decent-sized private room for around 50,000 won (just under US$50) per night. And since *gyul* (a fruit similar to a tangerine) grow in abundance on Jeju, *minbak* owners will sometimes give you as many as you can eat as part of the deal.

MAN-MADE ATTRACTIONS

The main city on Jeju, Jeju City, is not especially pretty. Instead, try Seogwipo, which is not far from Jungmun. Seogwipo is a surprisingly lively place, with a water park, plenty of bars, and even the World Eros Museum, which hosts a collection of erotic art from around the world. The World Eros Museum competes with Jeju Loveland, a park stuffed full of the most ridiculous sex-themed sculptures you have ever seen.

Thankfully there are other types of museum, including my personal favorite, the Chocolate Museum. There is also a Green Tea Museum, which isn't terribly exciting. Also check out the monument to Hendrick Hamel, a Dutch sailor who in 1653 became the first Westerner to land in Korea. He didn't intend to make such history—he and his crew-mates were shipwrecked, captured, and held in Korea until their escape in 1666.

THE BEST OF THE REST OF KOREA

A visit to the North Korean border is one of the essentials of a trip to South Korea. It is undeniably exciting to step into the negotiating room that lies half in one Korea and half in the other. Being stared down by North Korean officers is a little eerie, but rest assured that it is a lot worse for the soldiers stationed there who live like that every day.

The DMZ

There are several trips run from Seoul to the DMZ, but the "classic" (and best) one is operated by the USO, and should cost around 60,000 won. It is a tour from an American military point of view, but you do get to see all the important places—the negotiating room and the "bridge of no return," for instance. Lunch will be included in the price as well.

You can also take independent trips by simply driving to certain border points. If you head north from an east coast town named Goseong for instance, you'll reach the Unification Observatory, where you can peer into North Korea through binoculars. For me, the DMZ here looks even more tragic: because you are by the sea, you see a fenced-off beach, and a beautiful blue sea that stretches to the horizon. Seagulls, of course, freely fly in any direction they choose.

Clockwise from bottom left Seoraksan; military policemen at the DMZ; traditional entertainment at Andong; a wintry scene at Seoraksan National Park.

ANDONG

This is possibly the most conservative, traditional town in Korea. Queen Elizabeth II was taken there on her trip to Korea, after asking to be shown some history. Andong is famed for education, particularly of the Confucian variety. Legendary scholars like Yi Hwang (1501–70) made it their home, establishing schools there. One of the most historically powerful (and notorious) Korean clans, the Andong Kim, also hail from the town.

Visitors usually take in the traditional Hahoe Village, and see the famed Andong "Masked Dance." Food-wise, don't neglect to try *Andong jjimdak*, a braised soy-sauce based chicken stew with noodles and vegetables. And if you're a bit of a drinker, you'll be keen to check out the Soju Museum. Andong is famed for its traditional *sojus*, and the museum offers a tasting room.

GYEONGJU

A capital of the Silla Dynasty. Silla was a Buddhist kingdom, and thus the city is famous for temples, such as the impressive Bulguksa. A short trek up from Bulguksa is Seokguram Grotto, where a magnificent seated Buddha statue awaits the solstice: on that day, rays of sunlight hit the Buddha's "third eye" (in the forehead) and reflect in the direction of an old temple, now long since destroyed by the Mongols.

The national museum is worth visiting, for its wealth of Silla artifacts. And Gyeongju—and in particular, the area around Bomun Lake—is also a great place for cycling.

JEONJU

This is the capital of North Jeolla province, and the ancestral home of Yi Seonggye, the founder of the Joseon Dynasty. The pace of life is slow in Jeonju, and the people are friendly. The town is also known for a variety of foods: there is Jeonju-style *bibimbap* made with beef stock and bean sprouts; *kongnamul gukbap* (more bean sprouts and rice in a soup); and *dwaeji-gogi jeongol* (a kind of spicy pork stew).

There is also a tradition of *gamaek*, convenience-type stores setting up tables and selling beer and dried fish for customers. People use such shops just like bars.

Jeonju is also famous for its Hanok Village, where you may even stay in a *hanok* guesthouse. And if you go in late April–early May, you'll be able to catch the Jeonju Film Festival.

GANGWON-DO

This is a province to the east of Seoul. Its capital is Chuncheon, a pretty, relaxed town known for *dakgalbi* (spicy chicken stew). Close to Chuncheon is Namiseom, a popular tourist trap where romantic walks can be enjoyed. When I go to Chuncheon, I also take the short bus ride to Soyang Dam (the largest rock-filled dam in Asia) and then catch the boat to Cheongpyeongsa, an impressive Buddhist temple.

About fifty miles northeast of Chuncheon is Seoraksan, one of Korea's most beloved mountains. Seoraksan offers spectacular scenery, particularly in the autumn with the turning of the leaves. From Seoraksan, it is then just a short journey to the charming seaside town of Sokcho as well. And if by chance you are in the area on the fifth day of the fifth month of the lunar calendar (that will probably be some time in June), head to nearby Gangneung as well, where you can see the famed Danoje Festival. Danoje has been going for over a thousand years, and is full of traditional Korean games like Ssireum wrestling, shaman rituals, musical performances, and of course, plenty of *eumjugamu*.

> Bulguksa, perhaps Korea's most famous temple, in the city of Gyeongju. "Bulguksa" means "Buddha Country temple," in reference to the Silla state's commitment to Buddhism.

GETTING OFF THE BEATEN TRACK

Though a small country, there seems to be no end of places worth seeing in Korea. The owner of the "Chris in South Korea" blog, Chris Backe, lived here for several years and made a point of going to a different tourist attraction every weekend. He is in Thailand now, where he is having similar adventures—but his Korean blog is still online, and is an excellent way to discover all kinds of weird and wonderful places—such as the Suwon Toilet Museum!

I don't know as much as Chris does about off-the-beaten-track locations. But I can at least recommend the following as lesser-known attractions:

MAISAN

Not far from Jeonju lies Maisan, or "horse ear mountain." Really though, its more like two pointy peaks that do indeed resemble horses' ears. The main attraction though is the presence nearby of eighty small pagodas made entirely from pebbles, patiently built by Yi Gap-yong, a 19th century hermit. The overall effect is one of odd beauty. When traveling there, stay at the Red Ginseng Spa, a small and very chilled-out hotel and spa resort.

Top Map of South Korea. **Left** These two rocks resemble horses' ears when seen from a distance. **Below** A beautiful route going towards Tapsa temple at Maisan Mountain.

JEUNG-DO

This is an island off the coast of South Jeolla province, designated as a "slow" place; that means that you won't find a McDonalds, or even lights at night-time—Jeung-do has joined the International Dark Sky Association, so that you may go there and see the stars. The south side of the island has a 2.3 mile (4 km) long white sand beach named Ujeon. Jeung-do is becoming popular with Korean tourists though, so all that blissful slowness may not last forever.

Left Jeonju Hanok Village—Living Experience Center, Jeonju Hanok.

Right and below Jeonju Hanok Village

CHEOLLIPO

At Taean, south of Incheon, lies Cheollipo, one of the best arboretums in the world. Here, you can see over 13,000 different species of trees and plants. Cheollipo's creator was Carl Ferris Miller (Min Byeong-gal), an American who became a naturalized Korean, and ended up living here from 1953 until his death in 2002. Mr. Miller is himself worth reading up on, due to his long business career in Korea, and colorful personal life.

BOSEONG

This area is noted for its tea farms. I cannot imagine Korea without green tea, and this is where it is grown. There isn't much else to say, other than the fact that the plantations are strikingly beautiful and worth the journey.

Wawoojongsa Temple

There are over 3,000 Buddhist statues on the temple grounds, the most famous of which are the Buldu (Buddha heads) placed at the entrance and the Wabul (reclining Buddha statue) stationed in the middle of the mountain. The 26 feet (8 m) high Buldu is the largest of its kind and the Wabul, which is made from a juniper tree, is 10 feet (3 m) high and 39 feet (12 m) long. As the world's biggest wooden Buddhist sculpture, the Buldu has been registered in the Guinness Book of Records.

TONGYEONG

Tongyeong is a town rich in history, being the main base of Admiral Yi Sun-sin, Korea's greatest military hero. During the Imjin War of 1592–1598, Admiral Yi defeated the invading Japanese in 23 battles out of 23, despite a heavy numerical disadvantage.

Tongyeong also happens to be a beautiful coastal town. This makes it popular with Korean tourists, but as yet, foreign tourists don't usually make the trip. Tongyeong is well worth a visit, though.

Grand Tongyeong Bridge

Left View of Hallyeohaesang National Marine Park in Tongyeong, South Gyeongsang province.

Right Cafe in Dongpirang Village, Tongyeong.

SKIING IN KOREA

Before first coming here, I had the crazy misconception that Korea would be warm all year round. But temperatures from mid-December to late February can reach as low as minus 20 degrees Celsius. Frankly, I hate it. But if you love winter sports, my loss is your gain.

Korea is very mountainous. This and those cold, snowy winters make this country a great place for ski resorts. Large *chaebols* have naturally moved in to dominate the industry, developing sophisticated multi-purpose resorts with all the latest equipment, fancy ski-lifts, runs of all difficulty levels, luxury accommodation, and plenty of apres-ski entertainment options. And generally speaking, snowboarders and skiers are equally welcome.

THE MAIN SKI RESORTS

The oldest and biggest ski resort in Korea is Yongpyong Resort, Gangwon Province. It was founded in 1976 (which makes it ancient in South Korean terms) and features 28 different slopes. The longest and most famous of these is Rainbow, but Mega Green is the one most recommended for newbies.

Nearby is Alpensia, whose six slopes are known for their beginner-friendliness. The accommodation there is also impressive—it will be used to house athletes during the 2018 Winter Olympics.

But because Alpensia slopes aren't hardcore enough for the Olympics, the athletes themselves will be competing at Yongpyong and another nearby resort, Phoenix Park.

ALSO TRY THESE...

Also in Gangwon Province is the relatively new High1 Resort, which probably isn't as good as Yongpyong, but does have the advantage of being part of the Gangwonland Casino complex. This is the only casino in the whole country in which Koreans are legally allowed to play, giving the resort owners a license to print money.

North Jeolla province has Muju Resort, which according to popular expat publication *10 Magazine* has "the only real Nordic ski terrain in Korea," and is also "the most scenic of any ski resort in Korea." You can access Muju easily by rail. If you don't wish to travel that far, though, there is also Jisan Valley—which is in Gyeonggi province, very close to Seoul. Jisan Valley is also famed for its annual rock festival.

HOW MUCH DOES IT COST?

A day of skiing at a Korean resort, including equipment rental and transportation, should cost around 100,000 won. If you plan on staying longer, factor in accommodation as well—stay in a "love motel" for 40–50,000 won, or splurge hundreds of thousands on something more upmarket. These days, there are many cheap all-inclusive ski trip deals available on social commerce websites like Groupon, and local competitors TicketMonster, Coupang, and Wemakeprice.

A panoramic view of Yongpyong.

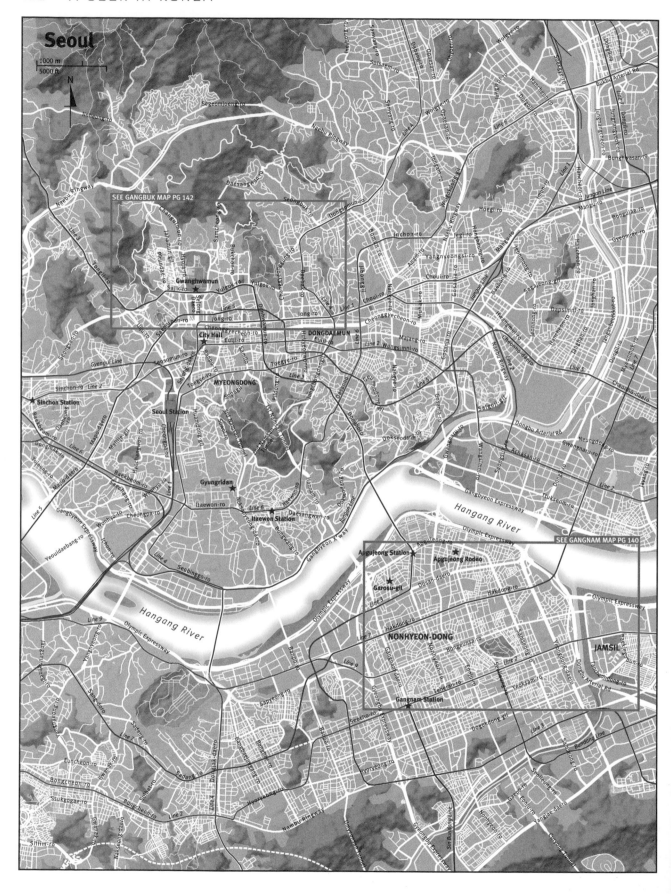

Seoul

GETTING AROUND BY PUBLIC TRANSPORT

With 50 million people squashed into an area the size of the US state of Kentucky, Korea couldn't get by without effective public transport. Thankfully, those living in any good-sized Korean city are blessed with an abundance of buses, underground trains, planes, and taxis. How do you get around in Korea? Let's look at the options.

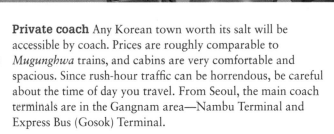

Trains Intercity trains in Korea are punctual, clean, and not particularly expensive. You can usually just show up on the day and buy your ticket, though you will certainly need to book around public holidays like Lunar New Year (*seollal*). There are several types of train—*Saemaeul* and *Mugunghwa* are the old and slow ones, while KTX is double the price and gets you there in half the time. *Mugunghwa* is my personal favorite—it has great legroom, and *noraebang* booths in the refreshments carriage.

Seoul Metro The Seoul Metro is an eighteen line, seven million passenger per day monster that manages to be clean, on time, and offer flawless cellular phone coverage. It is also quite cheap—standard journeys cost around US$1. It is without doubt the best way to get around Seoul and its satellite cities. Pay for your journey with a T-Money card, which can be purchased (and topped up) at the station. Ticket machines have English, Chinese, and Japanese instructions. Busan, Daegu, Gwangju, and Daejeon also have similar, but smaller, metro networks.

Public bus You can use your Seoul T-Money card on the bus, too. This is just as well, as they are usually crowded, and scratching around for the right change may earn you a lot of angry stares. There are green buses for local routes, and blue ones for city-wide routes. Red buses go even further, from Seoul to satellite city Bundang, for instance. Compared to the Metro, there is much less information available in foreign languages.

Flights Over-enthusiasm and "pork barrel" politics means that Korea has nine international airports, quite a lot for a small country. One of them, Yangyang, hosted just 6,000 passengers in 2011. But if you want to go from Seoul to Jeju Island, a flight from Gimpo Airport will get you there in an hour, and cost about US$50–60. And despite the best efforts of the local Korean Air/Asiana duopoly to keep them out, international low cost carriers like AirAsia are starting to take off in Korea, too.

Private coach Any Korean town worth its salt will be accessible by coach. Prices are roughly comparable to *Mugunghwa* trains, and cabins are very comfortable and spacious. Since rush-hour traffic can be horrendous, be careful about the time of day you travel. From Seoul, the main coach terminals are in the Gangnam area—Nambu Terminal and Express Bus (Gosok) Terminal.

Taxis Opinion is divided on Korean taxi drivers. Some see them as angry Michael Schumacher wannabes, who drive around in fare-raising circles at hair-raising speed. Others, like me, see them mostly as hard-working guys who will give you a good chat and get you where you need to be. A journey all the way across a big city like Seoul will cost about US$15–20. Cabs are plentiful in most areas. Be warned though, drivers rarely speak any language other than Korean—so prepare accordingly. The more of a tourist you appear, the greater the chance of an expensive detour.

Water taxis One company operates Seoul water taxis, which are a little-known method of getting from big residential area of Jamsil to financial district Yeouido, for US$5. The name "water taxi" does them a disservice—they're more like funkily-designed speedboats.

SHOULD YOU GO TO NORTH KOREA?

These days, a lot of people ask me about tourism in North Korea. I thought long and hard about the idea of including a short section on it here—after all, this is a book about the South. The two Koreas are of the same historic nation, but they are politically distinct and run in utterly different ways. But in the interests of answering people's queries, and providing a lesson in contrast, I concluded, why not?

There is, however, an important ethical question about traveling to North Korea. Some say that it just provides extra money to the government—which as everyone knows, is very brutal and oppressive. Others contend that despite that, tourism enables the ordinary North Koreans acting as hotel staff, guides, and bus drivers, to make a living. There is also the view that any kind of exchange in which North Koreans can meet people from other countries, and be exposed to outside ideas, is to be welcomed.

These are the factors you will have to weigh up when deciding whether or not to visit North Korea as a tourist. If you choose not to, then it is completely understandable. But if your choice is "yes," please read on.

GETTING AN "INVITE"

One does not just hop on a plane and fly to Pyongyang. Letters of invitation and visas are required—and unless you have solid connections or a silver tongue (in Chinese and/or Korean language), the only way you will get these is through middlemen. North Korea is a state governed by relationships rather than rules.

These middlemen aren't shadowy, hard-to-find operators. There are in fact a number of tour companies who have built up long-term relationships with the authorities, and can offer regular tour packages to North Korea. The most famous and respected is Koryo Tours, a group which has been in operation since 1993. Koryo is owned by two Englishman, and run from an office in Beijing. They supply North Korea with around half of its foreign tourists.

Firms like Koryo make the process a straightforward one. You may simply fill out a form via their website, along with a scanned image of your passport, and they will take care of the letter of invitation, and everything else.

Except under exceptional circumstances, all visitors will enter through China. The main ways in are via air from Beijing, or by train through the Chinese border town of Dandong. Air Koryo (no relation to Koryo Tours), North Korea's airline, operates regular flights between Beijing and Pyongyang's Sunan Airport. Air Koryo has the lowest possible flight safety rating, but it is equally true that "they haven't killed anybody yet," according to one recent tourist. Apparently the pilots fly in a "military" style—no-nonsense, and aggressive on landing.

WHAT YOU CAN SEE, AND WHAT YOU CAN'T

Foreign tourists to North Korea are assigned guides. Your guide is also a "handler," whose job it is to make sure you stay away from any place the authorities would not like you to see (slums, for instance). Tours are run along pretty regimented lines, and are full of sites related to the regime, such as the Kumsusan Memorial Palace in Pyongyang, where the preserved bodies of Kim Il-sung and Kim Jong-il await you as macabre tourist attractions.

The most popular tours center on the capital, Pyongyang, where it is possible

Above An Air Koryo plane at Beijing, being prepared for the flight to Pyongyang.

Top right Statue of Kim Il-sung.

to take a short subway ride, visit government-run shops and restaurants, see the War Museum, and go tenpin bowling. There are also tours timed for special events, such as the famous Arirang Mass Games, an eerily well-choreographed spectacle in which thousands of people dance in unison, in praise of the regime.

Moranbong Park should be a highlight, as you will see ordinary people doing ordinary things, such as picnicking, drinking, or playing games. Spring is the best time to enjoy this. The air is also very clean, due to the lack of industrialization. By many accounts, Pyongyang looks rather like a "third tier" Chinese city, before economic growth really took off.

Also, do not be surprised if you see conspicuous consumption in Pyongyang. To live in Pyongyang is a privilege in itself, and at the top of the pyramid are the high government officials, and the emerging capitalist class who conduct trade with China. They and their families do live well, buying up

Below Commuters traveling on the busy Pyongyang Metro, which is famed for being cut extremely deep into the ground—stations also double as bomb shelters.

Kumsusan Memorial Palace in Pyongyang, the resting place of Kim Il-sung and Kim Jong-il.

fancy cars, luxury brand clothes, and even iPads. It would be a foolish misconception to believe North Korea to be a properly socialist country in which everyone is equal.

These days, Pyongyang is just one option among many. Tour groups now offer trips to Baekdusan, the tallest mountain on the peninsula and the most important one in Korean folklore. It is also possible to see the east coast port city of Wonsan, where you may take a dip in the sea during the summer months. North Korea is also blessed with the natural beauty of Geumgangsan, a mountain which used to be accessible from the South through special agreement between the two countries. Today, you can only see it via tour groups like Koryo.

The country is clearly more open to foreign tourists than ever before. However, in absolute terms, it is still nowhere near "open." It is unlikely you would be allowed to leave your hotel and just wander freely. The tourist route is carefully controlled: you will rarely see litter, potholed roads, or even disabled people, for instance. In 2012, a bus driver accidentally took some visiting journalists into a run-down area of Pyongyang, where all three could be seen—and that in itself became a news story.

Right Man teaching his grandson to fish. **Below** A North Korean wedding. **Bottom** A Pyongyang street scene.

HANDLING YOUR HANDLER

One of the worst misconceptions about North Korea is that its people are robots. Though you will certainly hear robotic expressions of love for the regime, put yourself in their shoes: what do you think would happen to them if they said, "Well, Kim Jong-il wasn't all that great"? It may interest you to know that North Koreans generally liked Kim Il-sung, but not his son Kim Jong-il, who presided over famine and extreme mismanagement, as well as the customary brutality.

So when talking to your handler, treat them as a human being. And try to stay away from politics—you'll have a more interesting conversation that way. After all, "It's not usually socially acceptable to immediately start pushing people you don't really know on very deep and tough political questions," says regular North Korea visitor James Pearson. "Build up a good relationship with your guide by asking them about simple things like sports, food, family relations, and so on. What have they heard about your country? What's their favorite food? Favorite sport? All guides will have a university degree of some sort, so you can ask them about their student days, too. Like all North Koreans, they're really just normal people trying to do their job," he advises.

It is also a good idea to take gifts for your handler. Something representative of your country would be appropriate, but the ideal gift would probably be something saleable, like a bottle of whisky, or a carton of cigarettes. Your handler's wages will be pitiful, so such a gift would make a big difference.

Once you make friends with your handler, and they gain a degree of trust in you, you may find that their guard drops. Then, you can ask more searching questions—not so much about politics, but about ordinary life in North Korea. As in South Korea, people in the North like a drink, so see if you can have some Daedonggang Beer or *soju* with them.

James Pearson has also visited with an NGO, called the Pyongyang Project. His handler on that occasion, "asked me and my small group of NGO workers to 'remove our bibles from our luggage and leave them here at the border'. Puzzled, we explained that we didn't have any bibles. 'You mean you're not missionaries?' the guide immediately asked. [Most NGO visitors to Korea are Christian missionaries.] 'No,' we explained. The guide was so excited, largely because this meant we could smoke and drink together in the evenings." They drank so much that "the next morning, he wished we had been teetotal missionaries."

Mr. Pearson also has a funny story about one of his handlers. "When driving between Pyongyang and Kaesong [home of the joint North-South industrial complex] once, our group got off the bus to have a break by the side of the road. One of the group needed the toilet, and asked our guide if he could go by the side of the road. 'Yes of course,' the guide said. 'JUST WATCH OUT FOR THE LANDMINES!'"

Clearly, North Korea isn't an ordinary country by any stretch of the imagination. But it won't last forever, so those who are curious should try to see it sooner rather than later.

Above The bridge that links Dandong, China, to North Korea. Only a very narrow river separates the two countries, and at some points it is shallow enough to wade across.

Published by Tuttle Publishing, an imprint of
Periplus Editions (HK) Ltd.

www.tuttlepublishing.com

Text copyright © 2014 Daniel Tudor
Maps © 2014 Periplus Editions (HK) Ltd

ISBN: 978-0-8048-4384-3

Distributed by:

North America, Latin America
& Europe
Tuttle Publishing
364 Innovation Drive
North Clarendon
VT 05759-9436 U.S.A.
Tel: 1 (802) 773-8930
Fax: 1 (802) 773-6993
info@tuttlepublishing.com
www.tuttlepublishing.com

Japan
Tuttle Publishing
Yaekari Building, 3rd Floor
5-4-12 Osaki, Shinagawa-ku
Tokyo 141-0032
Tel: (81) 3 5437-0171
Fax: (81) 3 5437-0755
sales@tuttle.co.jp
www.tuttle.co.jp

Asia Pacific
Berkeley Books Pte. Ltd.
61 Tai Seng Avenue
#02-12
Singapore 534167
Tel: (65) 6280-1330
Fax: (65) 6280-6290
inquiries@periplus.com.sg
www.periplus.com

18 17 16 15 14
7 6 5 4 3 2 1

Printed in Singapore
1408CP

TUTTLE PUBLISHING® is
a registered trademark of
Tuttle Publishing, a division
of Periplus Editions (HK) Ltd.

The Tuttle Story
"Books to Span the East and West"

Many people are surprised to learn that the world's largest
publisher of books on Asia had its humble beginnings in the tiny
American state of Vermont. The company's founder, Charles
Tuttle, belonged to a New England family steeped in publishing.

Immediately after WW II, Tuttle served in Tokyo under General
Douglas MacArthur and was tasked with reviving the Japanese
publishing industry. He later founded the Charles E. Tuttle
Publishing Company, which thrives today as one of the world's
leading independent publishers.

Though a Westerner, Tuttle was hugely instrumental in bringing a knowledge of Japan and Asia to a world hungry for information about the East. By the time of his death in 1993, Tuttle had
published over 6,000 books on Asian culture, history and art—a
legacy honored by the Japanese emperor with the "Order of the
Sacred Treasure," the highest tribute Japan can bestow upon a
non-Japanese.

With a backlist of 1,500 titles, Tuttle Publishing is more active
today than at any time in its past—inspired by Charles Tuttle's
core mission to publish fine books to span the East and West and
provide a greater understanding of each.